PLEASE DON'T HURT ME

LEONARD KEENE

An indepth counseling session
demonstrating how to counsel people
who have been hurt deeply by others

BALANCED LIFE®

Association
P. O. Box 8159
Fort Worth, Texas 76112

I wish to dedicate this book to all the people who have been used of God in directing my paths. People like my parents, teachers, clients, friends and particularly my wife and family. People used of God to assist one another. People used of God to direct and teach me the ways of the Lord. To my Lord and my friends I dedicate this book.

CONTENTS OF SPECIAL THOUGHT NOTES

ABOUT THE AUTHOR

Leonard Keene is a graduate of the University of Oregon with degrees in Sociology, Business and Law. He holds a Doctor of Jurisprudence.

Leonard practiced law for ten years in Oregon before God called him into full time seminar teaching and ministry. In law practice and counseling he specialized in family conflicts, criminal law and the numerous problems of the individual.

Leonard was born and reared in Oregon. He served three years in the U. S. Army as a paratrooper and in police work.

Leonard has served on church boards, legal boards and Christian youth boards.

Leonard, Cloetta and their two children, Randy age 11, and Joetta age 9 now reside in Fort Worth, Texas. His expanding ministry now includes: A 15 hour Seminar on Balanced Living, individual teachings on Relationships, Parent-Child, Husband-Wife, Broken Relationships, Self-Image, Effective Counseling and other teachings God lays on his heart. He is also writing and teaching by audio tape.

Leonard and his family are living examples of the results of a Balanced Life.

INTRODUCTION

Why are people so unhappy? Recently I traveled with my wife, Cloetta and our two children, Randy and Joetta, on a holiday through the Eastern United States. As our Volkswagen bus chugged through the large cities with familiar names, New York, Washington D.C., Boston, and many others we began to notice the faces of the people.

People lost in large crowds. All in a hurry to go somewhere. But where? Why the hurry? How could they get so lost in such a large crowd? Are they really as lonely and hurt as they look?

Look at each face. Some are tense and drawn. Some are blank, with no emotion showing. Some have their faces twisted with an expression of pain; as a prizefighter in a boxing match awaiting another hit in the face.

Randy said, "Dad why are there so many unhappy people? They look like they have been 'hurt'. Is there something we can do for them?"

Jesus looked on the masses and saw the "hurts". He had compassion for them; for they were as sheep without a shepherd. No one to care for their hurts.

What is this book about? Healing the hurts of the people. Having compassion for them and doing something about it.

Randy and I decided to name these hurt people. We called them "Wounded Walkers". People who are up and around; walking, talking, working and playing but who are wounded. . .wounded deeply. They are "Wounded Walkers".

Proverbs 18:14 "The Spirit of a man will sustain his infirmity, but a wounded spirit who can bear?"

The "Wounded Walkers" have wounds in their spirit. The pain is unbearable to many. So unbearable that suicide is now a national disease. Even among professional counselors such as psychiatrists, suicide is a problem.

The inability to heal these wounds frustrates many a counselor. This book has been written to illustrate how these wounded spirits can be healed by God.

Leonard T. Keene

The intercom buzzed with a loud sense of urgency. "Mr. Keene, your 2:00 o'clock appointment is here". The receptionist declared as she moved her mouth closer to the large receiver to speak, "Shall I show her in?"

Before responding to the voice I thought to myself, is there no end to the problems? I wonder what this lady's difficulty will be.

Counseling is a painful process. In counseling, the root of the problem must be unearthed. Dug up. . . Exposing root problems in a person's life is painful. It must be done carefully so as not to cause a deeper hurt. I suppose it is painful because it is much like pulling the roots of a plant out of the ground. The unearthing of roots tears loose some dirt.

Perhaps that is why so many of us make such diligent effort to keep the root of our problems hidden from the view of others.

It's painful to change existing habits and behavioral patterns. Some roots must be disturbed while others must be torn out.

The writer, Paul, in Colossians speaks of putting off the OLD MAN and putting on the NEW MAN. It is painful but necessary. Happiness and peace of mind are at stake. Well, let's find out what is this lady's trouble.

1

"Cloetta, send her in."

As the door opened I looked up to see the new client. She was blonde and attractive. Very tall, perhaps 5'8", slim and well dressed. She moved toward my desk with a sense of sureness. She knew her purpose and her destination. I arose. The receptionist spoke, "Mr. Keene, I would like you to meet Sandra Lee, she has an appointment with you for 2:00 o'clock."

Sandra reached out to shake my hand. I responded by taking a firm hold. Her hand was warm and wet. Hands often tell inner feelings. Through the nervousness of her handshake, I could detect Sandra probably had much inner frustration. She was covering her inner frustrations well, except for her hands. Her hands gave her away.

I suppose this is true of most people. Their hands tell on them. Bitten off nails, nervousness, sweating, busy, calm or well groomed hands. All these tend to identify the person within.

"Sandra, I'm glad to know you. Will you be seated please?" indicating the chair in front of the desk.

"Cloetta, will you please stay? You can sit over here to my left," I added.

Sandra glanced toward me with a look of bewilderment and asked, "Mr. Keene, why is the receptionist staying?"

My response was to the point. "Her presence will prevent a number of traps from hindering our counseling session. Many people have been injured by failure to heed the warnings of the danger that exists between a male counselor and a female client. The receptionist's presence will help keep us on the correct path. The only alternative would be to have an aged lady counsel you. Much like Paul told Titus. 'You can counsel the aged men, you can counsel the young men, you can counsel the aged women, but you leave the young women alone'. Titus 2: 1-6. It is either this way or we'll have an aged woman counsel you."

"I understand," was Sandra's quick reply.

COUNSELING WOMEN

"Have you discussed this problem with your husband?" Many women who come for counseling have not discussed their problem with their husband. The reasons vary from "He won't listen" to "He wouldn't understand" or "I'm afraid of him."

Many divorce summonses served upon the husband by the Sheriff or process server are a surprise to the husband. This ought not to be. One of the primary goals of the counselor should be to prepare the wife to discuss the problem openly and in a spirit of love with her husband. She should be instructed not to say: "Mr. Keene says. . . thus and so. . ." This type of comment brought home to the husband by the wife after a counseling session will only add "gasoline" to an existing fire. It is rejection by implication. . . I reject you, I accept my counselor as my model.

She is saying, "I approve of Mr. Keene (the counselor) and I want you to be like him."

The husband often interprets these comments as rejection by the wife. He is hurt. He then will either turn away, spending his spare time on airplanes, boats, motorcycles, extra work or other women. Or, he will explode—lashing out at the unseen counselor who is stealing the admiration of his wife.

I leaned back into my chair and asked, "Tell me about your problem, Sandra."

3

"Well, it is not really my problem. It is my husband. He is really the problem."

"In what way is your husband the problem," I responded.

"He shuts me out of his life. He works hard. When he comes home, he turns on the television, and begins to read the newspaper. He won't talk to me. When I speak to him or try to tell him my feelings, he won't listen. Mr. Keene, he just won't listen to me. I've tried to talk to him at bedtime but he says, 'Save it until morning, Sandra'. In the morning he is too busy to listen," she ended with a deep sigh.

"Has this always been the case between you and he?" I asked.

"Yes," she replied as she settled back into her chair.

"I noticed from the Information Sheet your husband, Richard is 27 years old, and you are 23. You have been married for two years. What was it like the first year of your marriage?"

I slid the information sheet forward so that it was more visible for my reference.

THE INFORMATION SHEET

This sheet should be filled out before you talk with the client concerning their problem. The information sheet will prepare you with much needed information and it will also prepare the client for the painful process of exposing personal information to a stranger.

INFORMATION SHEET

DATE 11-30-74

NAME Sandra Lee ADDRESS 521 Riverside

CITY Fort Worth STATE Tx ZIP 76112 PHONE 451-5656

OCCUPATION house wife - part time dress shop clerk

SEX F DATE OF BIRTH 4-10-51 WEIGHT 120 HEIGHT 5'7"

MARITAL STATUS yes

EDUCATION AND TRAINING High school - 3 years college

MY HEALTH IS (GOOD) AVERAGE POOR DECLINING

MY PRESENT ILLNESSES INCLUDE none

MY PHYSICIAN Dr. Hibbs

ARE YOU PRESENTLY TAKING MEDICATION no WHY

HAVE YOU EVER HAD A SEVER EMOTIONAL UPSET yes WHEN 2nd yr college

HAVE YOU EVER HAD ANY PSYCHO-THERAPY OR COUNSELING no

IF YES LIST COUNSELOR AND DATES

CIRCLE ANY OF THE FOLLOWING WORDS WHICH BEST DESCRIBE YOU
AT PRESENT

(ACTIVE)	PERSISTENT	SELF-CONSCIOUS	(EXTROVERT)
AMBITIOUS	NERVOUS	(USED-BY-OTHERS)	LONELY
SELF-CONFIDENT	(HARDWORKING)	(IMPATIENT)	MOODY
IMAGINATIVE	GOOD-NATURED	IMPULSIVE	(OFTEN BLUE)
(SUBMISSIVE)	EASY-GOING	INTROVERT	(EXCITABLE)
(LIKEABLE)	QUIET	SENSITIVE	CALM
SERIOUS	SHY	LEADER	HARD-BOILED

OTHER

PAGE 1

5

NAME OF SPOUSE _Richard Lee_ ADDRESS _same_
OCCUPATION OF SPOUSE _traveling salesman_ (on the road several days a month)
IS SPOUSE WILLING TO COME FOR COUNSELING _maybe_
HAVE YOU EVER BEEN SEPARATED OR FILED FOR DIVORCE _no_
IF YES DATE _____
DATE OF THIS MARRIAGE _6-10-72_
GIVE BRIEF INFORMATION ABOUT ANY PREVIOUS MARRIAGE
_____

CHILDREN:

NAME	AGE	SEX	LIVING YES-NO	EDUCATION IN YEARS	MARITAL STATUS
none	___	___	___	___	___
___	___	___	___	___	___
___	___	___	___	___	___
___	___	___	___	___	___

IF YOU WERE REARED BY ANYONE OTHER THAN YOUR OWN PARENTS,
BRIEFLY EXPLAIN _____
RATE YOUR PARENTS MARRIAGE UNHAPPY __ AVERAGE **X** HAPPY __
                            VERY HAPPY __
AS A CHILD DID YOU FEEL CLOSEST TO YOUR FATHER__ MOTHER**X** OTHER__
AS YOU SEE IT, WHAT IS THE MAIN PROBLEM _my husband_
and I can't communicate
WHY ARE YOU HERE _I want help - I want to be_
happy and have a successful marriage

PAGE 2

As Sandra glanced toward the information
sheet she had filled out previously, she began to
tell me about her husband, Richard.

"We have always had difficulty communicating.
Even from the start. He just will not let me get close
to him. Do you know what I mean? If I get too close
to the 'real Richard' he shuts me off. When he shuts
me off I feel hurt, and rejected. As you can see Mr.

Keene from the information sheet, Richard travels some, and is away from home several days a month. I used to look forward to his coming home. I would be excited about his arrival.

I'd also be sad when he left on his business trips. But recently it is almost the reverse. I get so I'm glad he is gone. It is a relief to see him walk out the door to begin one of his three or four day business trips. Actually I don't think I love him any more.

I haven't told Richard, but I've even begun thinking about a divorce. I know divorce is wrong, but I don't know what else to do."

IMBALANCE

Everything about God's creation is designed for balance. It seems that most animals, trees and insects are pre-programed to maintain this balance. It is only man who has been given such choice that he can violate God's system of balance at will.

I can remember, as a boy of 10 years, watching a squirrel carry acorns by the dozens to his hole in the tree. He was programed to store food for one winter. The little squirrel was completely engrossed in his preparation for "hard times" when the snow fell. He was also programed to know just how many acorns would get him through the winter. No more, No Less. But on the other hand it is man, who with a free will and a choice, decides to begin storing "acorns" (money, property and influence) for two years, five years, twenty years and one hundred years ahead.

Once man gets his "extra acorns" deposited in the tree he becomes fear oriented. . . fearful that others will come and steal his advanced supply. He becomes unbalanced by his over-concern for "acorn security" in the future.

I have found many of the problems facing the counselor is an unbalanced person sitting across the desk.

7

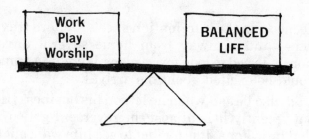

He tends to overdo one of the above or leave one or more completely out of his life. A person who works without play and worship is headed for problems. He is out of balance.

Many people work and play but fail to worship. That inner desire to worship is never met.

"Sandra," I replied, "Did you love Richard when you married him two years ago."

"Oh, yes," she answered.

"Sandra, before we go further in this counseling session, I want to show you something concerning successful counseling. You need to understand the things I'm about to show you before we can solve your problem.

Counseling is not a panacea. Counseling is not a cure-all. It is only a method of locating, cleaning, applying medication, and dressing the wound; so to speak. I call it a Band-Aid program. I can only LEAD YOU into solving your own problem. I can show you how to obtain the surgery that is necessary to ROOT OUT a difficulty. But I can't do it for you. Do you understand what I'm saying?"

Sandra leaned forward on the arms of her chair with interest and replied, "Yes, Mr. Keene, I believe I do understand. You are saying that it is sort of like leading a horse to water. He has to be the one that drinks for himself."

"Right! Counseling is a delicate balance

between the client discovering her problem and the counselor revealing the truth as he sees it. I call this delicate balance the SHOW AND TELL scales. Let me draw a picture of the scales on this chalkboard."

As I moved toward the chalkboard on the easel by my desk I added, "I like to draw diagrams and pictures. We tend to think in pictures.

"The difficulty with most counseling is the client spends most of her time on the show side of the balance. The counselor insisting the client discover all her own problems by a series of counseling sessions. Whereby the client ventilates by telling all of her inner most problems. As she hears herself talk out what is on the inside, she begins to discover her problem. As she discovers her problem through her own speaking, the counselor should begin guiding by telling the truth regarding correct human behavior. The client shows by talking, then a process of discovery takes place within her.

"At the same time the counselor from time to time tells by revealing the truth in love. Do you see this balance Sandra?

9

SHOW | TELL

Client discovery | Counselor tells Truth In Love

SHOW AND TELL

The Classical method of counseling is too heavy on the Show side of the scales. He lets the client talk, hours, days, weeks, months, years until she vents and Shows all that is within her. But not much tell by the Counselor. "Should I stop sleeping with different men?"

"Well it depends. Tell me more. . . ." Too much Show. Not enough tell. They have so little truth to tell they simply keep quiet and listen.

The Religious counselor tends to be heavy on the tell. The client shows for ten minutes and the counselor bursts forth with a 30 minute tell of SHOULDS and OUGHTS.

He too is out of balance on the tell. The client is not given sufficient time to show.

"As you begin to talk and disclose personal things about your life you will find yourself tending to discover problem areas. I will from time to time reveal the truth to you regarding your problem. We will attempt together to strike a correct level on the show and tell balance. Do you agree with the use of this principle in our counseling session today?"

Sandra smiled at Cloetta, looked back at me and said, "Yes, sir, I do agree."

BUILD THE RELATIONSHIP

Many people who come for help have been hurt and betrayed by intimate associates. Perhaps a husband or a wife has been disloyal. A best friend, employer, relative, pastor, parent or a child. . . someone has hurt the client. In the first and second hour of the session, carefully allow a relationship to develop that sounds of loyalty and trustworthiness. I Thessalonians 2:11 tells us how.

"As ye know how we EXHORTED and COMFORTED and CHARGED everyone of you as a father doth his children."

To EXHORT means to teach and show the truth. If the clients knew the truth, they would not likely be seeking your help. It may be they know right from wrong, but they may not know how acting on that knowledge will become truth, and set them free. It is up to you to guide truth into their lives as a father doth his children.

To COMFORT means to show in your attitude, action, and words "I care about you" "I'm here to suffer with you and to help you reduce that suffering." The greater the crowd the more people will be suffering; Jesus discerned this as he ministered to the thousands. The Bible says he was moved with compassion, for they had no shepherd. A shepherd examines his sheep for wounds and 11 hurts. He then ministers to those sheep that are suffering. At least for a short time the counselor becomes the shepherd to the "wounded sheep" he is counseling.

Don't be a HEAD NODDER. Some people in counseling get you to agree with a few fundamentals. As you agree and nod your head, you'll nod in agreement when they try to convince you their behavior is right, and everyone else is wrong. Don't be a Head Nodder.

To CHARGE means to let the client know he must act. He must do something to help recover himself out of his suffering.

II Timothy 2:24-26 "And the servant of the Lord (the counselor) must not strive; but be gentle unto all men, (the client) apt to teach, patient, in meekness instructing those that oppose themselves; (the client) if God peradventure will give them repentance to the acknowledging of the truth; And that they (the client) may recover themselves (the client) out of the SNARE (the place of continuing injury) of the devil, who are taken captive by him at his will."

Let the client discover that you have no secret formula or immediate cure-all for his problem. But you are willing to teach, love and help him recover from his place of suffering. A relationship between client and counselor builds. No betrayals. . .

Step number one: Build the relationship by exhorting, by comforting and by charging as a father doth his children.

"Tell me Sandra, has your husband ever had a close relationship with anyone in his life?" I asked.

Sandra thought for a minute then answered, "No, I imagine our relationship is his closest one."

"What about his parents? Tell me about his father and mother."

"Well, Richard's father was an alcoholic. I don't

know too much about him, except that he gave his family a pretty bad time. He is supposed to be somewhere in Oregon. Actually I have never seen him. Richard doesn't like to talk about his Dad. He says he doesn't hate him, he just doesn't like him. Just as he doesn't like cottage cheese. However, Richard's mother is a sweetheart. She worked and raised Richard, his brother, and sister. Richard does have a pretty close relationship with his mother and his brother."

"Sandra, is there anyone else your husband dislikes?" I asked.

"I don't think so," she replied, "he is really a pretty friendly guy. He is one of his company's top salesmen. Oh, wait, there is one old buddy who betrayed Richard by lying to other friends. That was way back in high school though. I suppose Richard dislikes this old buddy.

"Mr. Keene what are you probing for? What are you trying to get to? Is there something here that I'm missing?" Sandra asked nervously.

"Yes, Sandra, there is and I can illustrate by showing you a BROKEN RELATIONSHIP and its consequence. Suppose Mr. A and Mr. B are communicating and as a result of that interaction, A gets hurt and begins to dislike B. Let's draw another diagram." Reaching the chalkboard I erased the last diagram.

A   B

Sandra spoke quietly, "Mr. Keene, could I have some paper so I can take notes and also draw some of the diagrams?"

Cloetta opened a drawer near her and handed a small stack of paper and a pen to Sandra.

"The hurt that was created by the interaction caused a dislike or hatred in Mr. A. This breaks the relationship between A and B. A has a broken relationship with B. They may still work together, they may still see one another, but none the less there is a broken relationship. We can identify this broken relationship by inserting a bolt of bitterness across the communication flow between Mr. A and Mr. B."

A   **B**

"But, Mr. Keene, what is so strange about a broken relationship? There are many broken relationships. Doesn't everybody have broken relationships?" Sandra appeared puzzled.

"Many people do Sandra. But watch the next step. Mr. A now leaves the presence of Mr. B and goes to meet Mr. X.

Mr. A cannot completely keep his attention on Mr. X because his mind and emotions are still fixed upon Mr. B and the broken relationship. Mr. A cannot successfully relate to Mr. X because of the broken relationship. This broken relationship hinders his ability to deal successfully with Mr. X."

A   X

Sandra arose and walked toward the chalkboard as she spoke, "I still don't quite understand how a broken relationship can effect a person's ability to deal with other people?"

"Sandra, do you believe in God?" I asked.

"Yes", she replied as she sat down in her chair.

"Sandra, have you accepted Jesus as your Savior?"

"Yes," she replied again with a more determined ring in her voice.

"Now, one more question. Do you believe in the Bible?"

"Oh, yes, how could anyone not believe in the Bible," she declared.

"I John 2: 9, 10 and 11 holds the secret to understanding broken relationships and how they work. Here let me read it to you."

Reaching toward the corner of my desk, I picked up my Bible. The old Bible was beginning to become frayed around the edges. I thought of the new one in the drawer, but didn't really want to retire this old treasure.

Turning to I John I began to read, " 'He that saith he is in the light, and hateth his brother, is in   15 darkness even until now. He that loveth his brother abideth in the light, and there is none occasion of stumbling in him. But he that hateth (or dislikes) his brother is in darkness, and walketh in darkness, and knoweth not wither he goeth, because that darkness hath blinded his eyes.'

"Notice the verse says HE THAT HATETH IS BLINDED. We can call this blindness a BLINDSPOT. Something you can't see. A good illustration would be similar to driving an automobile. Suppose I am in the right hand lane and I decide to move into the left hand lane. I look in the mirror to check the traffic to my side. I see nothing. It all appears clear. It looks safe for me to change lanes; so I commence making my lane change. 'BEEP-BEEP' a horn to my left blares out. I swerve back to my lane. How did that car get beside me? I looked but didn't see him. He was in my blind spot. The danger was there all the time, I just did not see it.

BLINDSPOTS

16

"This is much the same with broken relationships. The danger is there, but we are blinded by the broken relationship. We have a blind spot.

"One more illustration. When I was in the Army I was on the boxing team. I soon learned how to win some of the prize fights. Simply do something during the boxing match that would irritate my opponent. He would soon become irritated and very angry with me. As he became angry, he would begin losing his ability to deal wisely in the boxing match. He soon began to swing wildly. He received blindspots from his hatred and dislike for me. All I had to do to defeat this opponent was to wait for his wild punch. As he swung wildly, I would move in with a well placed blow to the head. He would be on his way to defeat. Defeated because of the blindspots caused by his broken relationship with me.

"Broken relationships cause blindspots which stop us from acting wisely."

THE FIVE BASIC RELATIONSHIPS

Most people have at least five basic relationships. Each relationship is different and requires separate attention.

1. God ← – – – – – – – → Self
2. Self ← – – – – – – – → Self
3. Husband ← – – – – – → Wife
4. Parent ← – – – – – – → Child
5. Self ← – – – – – – → Others

A broken relationship on any level will show up in the other levels. For example. If a man has a broken relationship at work with a boss or co-worker, that 17 broken relationship will show up in the way he treats his wife and family. He may not realize he has changed, but his wife and children can tell you. Life is not as enjoyable for them.

If this man does not act promptly to heal the original broken relationship at work, it will cause other relationships to break. Perhaps he abuses his wife and this fosters further hurt. Most certainly the broken relationship is going to effect his ability to communicate with God.

We have a policy at our house—Don't break a relationship. It's not worth the cost you pay. Remember a broken relationship in one area will effect all other areas of relationships. Guard against the "BOLT OF BITTERNESS."

DEFINITION OF BROKEN RELATIONSHIPS. . .

When two or more people interact, hate, fear, resentment, jealousy, bitterness, unforgiveness, or anger rises up within the heart of one or more of the people involved.

Sandra's face flushed red as excitement arose within her. "Boy! Do you mean to tell me the reason Richard is not able to treat me correctly is because of the broken relationship he has with his father? Do I understand correctly what you are saying about the effects of broken relationships,

Mr. Keene? Richard does not realize he is treating me badly? Is that a correct observation?"

I leaned back in my chair with a warm sense of satisfaction sweeping through my spirit and returned, "You are learning fast."

Sandra continued, "But how do we get Richard to fix these broken relationships with his father and former friend if he does not realize how it's hurting both himself and me?"

"Sandra, we will handle that question later. First we must apply this to you!"

"What do you mean, apply this to me?" she responded.

"You do recall telling me a few moments ago you felt you no longer love Richard. Right?" I asked.

Sandra responded by a nod of her head.

"Let me ask you this? What would be the most harmful thing that you could do to Richard if you wanted to hurt him?"

"Stop loving him I suppose," she said rather quietly, "Take away my love from him."

"Often Sandra, when we are hurt and injured by other people it is natural to react by stopping our flow of love to that person. It often becomes an automatic reaction to injury. If someone hurts me, I will automatically stop my flow of love toward that person. They no longer deserve my love. That is our thinking so therefore, we stop the flow of love."

"Mr. Keene! Do you think my feelings of no love for Richard was a reaction to his injury to me? That I am just returning hurt for hurt?" she replied with a near frightened look on her face.

"It is an easy trap to fall into Sandra."

Sandra started to speak again, "Why couldn't I see it before I came for counseling? Do I have 19 blindspots? Oh, my goodness, if I have blindspots, that means I have broken relationships."

I walked to the door and opened it. Looking back at Cloetta I asked, "Could you bring us three cups of coffee? I think we are going to need it."

Cloetta asked before leaving the room, "Do you use cream or sugar, Sandra?"

Sandra shook her head no; then went on talking. "I don't think I have a broken relationship with anyone. Well, maybe. . . . I used to date a guy. His name was Buddy. But that was three or four years ago. It still wouldn't bother me now. . .would it?"

I returned to my chair and began to answer her question, "Broken relationships get worse as the years pass. I've known people who still had the effects of broken relationships 42 years later. . . still harboring the bitterness and resentment of the broken relationship. Broken relationships usually are what make the retirement years (the so-called Golden Years) so unpleasant for many people. Time does not heal broken relationships. Let me repeat, time does not heal broken relationships.

ROOTS OF BITTERNESS

Roots of bitterness are the result of hurts and wrongs done to us by others. If a person responds incorrectly to a hurt or wrongdoing, a root of bitterness is established within his or her personality. This bitterness will spring up, troubling both the person harboring the bitterness and also defiling many others. Put another way, bitterness within a person is a polluting agent that defiles people in the immediate environment.

Watch how easy it is to fall into line and agree when a man at a social gathering begins to criticize and speak out hate toward a person not in attendance. It's so simple to agree with that criticism and to begin to develope a similar root of bitterness in yourself.

You become convinced that the absent person has wronged you also. Hebrews 12:14-15 says "Follow peace with all men, and holiness, without which no man shall see the Lord; Looking diligently lest any man fail of the grace of God; lest any root of bitterness springing up trouble you, and thereby many be defiled."

A husband and wife can "taste the bitterness" in the attitude, speech, and conduct of one another. It pollutes the environment (the home and children).

Balanced Life Counseling is aimed at eradicating this bitterness so people can truly "open up to one another—submit to one another—love one another" in a meaningful way.

ROOTS OF BITTERNESS

"I'll be showing you the proper therapy for healing broken relationships a little later in this counseling session. But we still need to discover more of the root problem and learn more truth."

Picking up my Bible I turned back to Hebrews 12: 14 and 15.

"Notice this verse. 'Follow peace with all men, and holiness, without which no man shall see the Lord: Looking diligently lest any man fail of the grace of God; lest any root of bitterness springing up trouble you, and there many be defiled'.

"Roots of bitterness from broken relationships spring up quickly, without warning. . . thus troubling you and defiling many others."

The door opened behind Sandra, and Cloetta came in quietly. She set a cup of steaming coffee in front of Sandra and handed me another. She slipped back into her chair quickly.

Sandra asked, "Mr. Keene, may I tell you something very personal?"

"Yes, Sandra you may," I answered.

"Well, when Richard rejects me," Sandra paused as if trying to make certain what came out was right. "Like. . . when I need to talk to him so desperately, I think my insides are going to come apart. I try to pull him from his television program and he either ignores me. . . pretends to listen, but doesn't." Sandra paused, fighting back the tears. "He just tells me to leave him alone. I feel so rejected. I feel so all alone. And do you know what flashes into my mind?. . . A gray image of Buddy. You know, the old boy friend. Sometimes he is sneering at me. Sometimes he is trying to hurt me. Sometimes he is just standing there with a blank stare. I get a sick feeling down in the pit of my stomach.

"I wonder if this image flash of Buddy is a root of bitterness? Do you think it is a root of bitterness that is described in the verse you just read? Do I really have resentment, unforgiveness, and bitterness toward Buddy?

"Boy. . . the more I talk. . . the more I believe I do have a broken relationship with him. I tried to forgive him for the wrongs he did to me. I thought I had forgiven him. But I can see now that there is still unforgiveness down in my spirit. I am still hurt by the way he treated me. He hurt me and I still haven't gotten over it."

"Yes Sandra, and when Richard rejects you, he hurts you. That old root of bitterness springs up troubling you and affecting others.

"Unforgiveness can only be eradicated by an act of your will to forgive, PLUS, a SPIRITUAL HAPPENING on the inside. Simply an act of willing forgiveness is not always enough. You need help to pull up the roots of bitterness caused by the broken relationship."

Before I could go on, Sandra broke in, "Mr. Keene, I want to get this thing out of my system. I don't want to live this way any longer. Life is not getting better. . . life is getting worse. I must find the answer. I am too young and I want a happy life. Not one filled with bitterness."

NEED OF COUNSEL

"Without counsel, purposes are disappointed; but in the multitude of counselors they (the purpose) are established." Proverbs 15:22.

There are a lot of Lone Ranger Christians running about today doing their own thing. . . Accountable to no one. "It's just me and Jesus" they burst forth with a spirit of rebellion in their attitude. "I'll not have anyone tell me what to do".

Be careful Mr. Lone Ranger Christian, as one brother said, "God may take your gun, shoot your horse, and send your saddle home."

God seems to be saying to Christians everywhere, open up, submit yourselves to one another, you need the strength and security of a multitude of counselors. Get yourself a Shepherd. Become a

Shepherd. Get into a sheep fold before the storm comes. We need one another to assist in working out our imperfections and hang-ups. God is beckoning on the one hand with commitment, loyalty and obedience. Satan is beckoning on the other hand with rebellion, oppression, promise breaking, and doing your own thing. God's road leads to success and peace; Satan's road leads to failure and conflict.

"Sandra have you heard the story of John the Baptist and how he was beheaded by King Herod at the request of a dancing girl and her mother? The story is found in the Bible in Matthew, Chapter 14.

"At that time John and Jesus were best friends. John had been the one who baptized Jesus. John was in a special relationship with our Lord. What do you suppose Jesus felt when he learned of the death of his best friend? Particularly when he discovered the uselessness of John's death. John was killed because of the plotting evilness of a mother and daughter, who tricked the King into making an oath, to give the daughter her request. What was her request? John's head on a serving tray! When Jesus learned of this, he departed into a desert and the people followed him.

"It would have been easy for Jesus to have allowed unforgiveness to rise up at that time. It would have been easy to tell the people to go away, so he could be alone in his grief over the death of his best friend. But Jesus did not respond to the hurt that way. Instead, verse 14 says 'And Jesus went forth and saw a great multitude, and was moved with compassion toward them.'

"What followed was three miracles in the ministry of Jesus. He healed the sick, he multiplied fish and bread to feed thousands, and he walked on the water. Three of the great miracles Jesus performed were right after he RESPONDED CORRECTLY to the hurt done to him by the death of John.

"Now Sandra, notice carefully the sequence of events. . .

"Number One: The wrong done to Jesus (murder of his friend)

"Number Two: A correct response to the wrong

"Number Three: The miracles followed

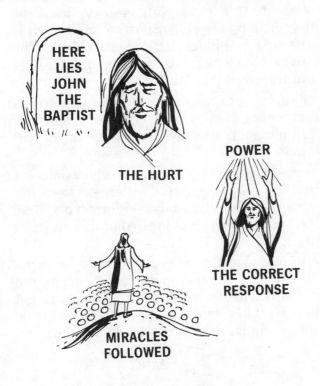

THE HURT

THE CORRECT RESPONSE

MIRACLES FOLLOWED

"Notice again. The wrong done, the correct response to the wrong; and then miracles followed. And we wonder why we as Christians are so helpless. We have not responded correctly to wrongs and hurts. If we would learn to respond 25 correctly, the miracles would follow our lives."

"I see it! I see it! I see!" Sandra blurted out. She reached over taking the hand of Cloetta, as she sat in silence for the next few moments. The awareness of this truth was sinking deep into her spirit. An expression of joy began to shine from her face. We all sat there silently for a few moments. I did not want to spoil the moment of truth for Sandra by more conversation.

As we sat silently, I thought to myself. . . The next step in this counseling session must be delicately lead by the Holy Spirit. A key principle in counseling is hidden in Proverbs 14:10 "The heart knoweth his own bitterness, and a stranger doth not intermeddle with his joy."

People get a certain joy from their own bitterness (Unforgiveness toward others). The "I hate her and I'll not stop because it feels good to me" Syndrome.

How many clients have I found who would not give up their resentment and bitterness toward a father, mother, church member, or former business partner, because there was joy in maintaining that bitterness.

I can remember the 35 year old preacher, who was so hurt by another pastor, that he began plotting ways to get even; plotting ways to get revenge. He later told me, he actually enjoyed mentally visualizing, how he would hurt him back.

How he would take a gun and blow his head off. Or like the husband or wife who nourish and cherish their bitterness caused by the other in time past. . . Continually bringing up old faults because there is joy in remembrance. A counselor must recognize that people get joy from their own bitterness. We must also recognize that a stranger doth not intermeddle with that joy.

We are strangers to the heart of the client. It is natural for the heart of the client filled with bitterness, to exclude all others from looking in. . . to exclude all strangers from intermeddling. Why? Simply because of the shame attached to exposure. Exposure of the insides of that person. Often if clients in frustration and panic are encouraged to let the counselor look too quickly on the inside. . . hatred for the counselor, by the client, will be the result. A stranger intermeddled with the joy of the heart's bitterness. The client may turn his bitterness toward the counselor. Instead of eradicating the bitterness, there is now even more bitterness.

THE SUFFERING HEROINE

Jamie, age 27 years, was divorced three years ago. It was a stormy marriage and a bitter separation. The court case with lawyers, counselors, judges and relative interference was a nightmare. Now it's all over. Jamie says to herself, "Never again will I allow myself to be exposed to such hurt and misery. From now on it's just Todd and me."

Todd is Jamie's son, age 4 years.

Jamie reasons to herself "I'll not allow Todd to be hurt like I was hurt. Life will be better for him. . .I'll see to it."

Jamie begins to take on an attitude determined to insulate Todd from injury of the world . . . at her 27 *own expense. In fact she says, "I don't care what it costs me, or how much I give up. Todd is going to have a good life."*

Jamie is becoming a suffering heroine. She is a heroine (in her own eyes) by laying her life down for her son. She is suffering and will soon let all of the audience watching her act, know that she is suffering.

She plays the role of the gallant and might, think-only-of-Todd-mother.

What's the promise? Life will get more unpleasant for Jamie. Her attitude and role playing as a suffering heroine, will deter the development of any genuine friendship. She will become more lonely. . . more bitter. When Todd reaches adulthood, Jamie may develop illnesses that will assist in holding Todd to an unspoken commitment.

You see, Todd owes his mother a great deal for her having sacrificed her life and happiness for his welfare. Todd may feel guilt about establishing his own life. There are many "Jamies" and many "Todds" at various stages of this game called. . . becoming a suffering heroine.

What is Jamie saying by her conduct? "I want two things from you. Feel sorry for me and don't get close to me, you may hurt me."

It requires a great deal of patience in counseling the Jamies and Todds. They both must be schooled and motivated to develope other close relationships.

The old hurt from the previous relationship hinders building new friends. With this in mind, it is often necessary to follow the steps to remove the hurt as will be demonstrated in Sandra's case.

The heart knows its own bitterness. She knows where her problem is rooted. It then becomes necessary to let her "discover it" and in general terms, confess the fault of bitterness to the counselor. I have found that it is not necessary to have the client tell me all the details.

In Sandra's case the fact that her old boyfriend, Buddy, had wronged her was sufficient confession on her part to begin the spiritual healing that will be necessary.

A counselor often falls into the trap of listening to, and encouraging discussion of intricate details of the wrong doing of the client. . .or details of the wrong done to the client. There is a large segment of the counseling world that practices such full and deep disclosure. I recommend against it for several reasons.

(1) Reliving the sexual assaults, the promiscuity, the sex play, the wrongful conduct in detail. . . often creates new injuries, wounds, and guilt.

(2) Intimate details activate the perverse nature of man. . . his body lust. . . lust of the eye, and greed on the part of the counselor.

(3) Counselor and client reliving every detail is much like seeing an "X" rated movie.

(4) Ephesians 5:11-13 "And have no fellowship with the unfruitful works of darkness, but rather reprove them. For it is a shame even to speak of those things which are done of them in secret. But all things that are reproved are made manifest by the light: for whatsoever doth make manifest is light."

Such detail becomes permanently imprinted on the mind of all persons present. What counselor is able to sit 6 to 10 hours a day watching "X" rated movies and still maintain his sanity? How can he expect to walk in the spirit and not lust after the things of the flesh?

I suppose the very fact so many counselors listen to and encourage the discussion of gory details is why the psychiatrists have a large percentage of suicide. The human mind and spirit cannot bear

29

the continual supply of perverse thoughts.

For this same reason many active pastors in churches get side tracked. There becomes a focus on the things of the flesh, rather than a focus on the things of the spirit.

Sandra had begun to relax and enter into a new state of peace.

"Are you ready to begin the steps to get the hurt out?" I stood, to prepare myself, to write again on the chalkboard.

"Yes Mr. Keene, I am ready," Sandra looked up smiling and released Cloetta's hand.

Cloetta smiled, and slid a few more sheets of paper to Sandra, to be sure she had an ample supply.

"Alright, here goes," Speaking as I began writing.

"Step Number 1: See yourself through the eyes of the wrongdoer."

"Examine your own response to the wrongdoer's behavior. What problem did Buddy have that affected the way he treated you? Did Buddy have broken relationships? If he did, he may not have realized he was treating you incorrectly. He may have been blinded by broken relationships with his father, mother or some other person. Remember, Sandra, blindspots often cause bad behavior. This bad behavior is easily interpreted by others as selfishness.

He may not realize he was acting selfishly. He may have been blinded to the real significance of his acts and how they hurt you."

"Whow! I never thought of it that way. You mean to tell me, that he may not have realized that he was hurting me?" Sandra asked.

"That's correct. He still may not realize he wronged you," I replied. "Let's go on to the second step."

"Step Number 2: Re-examine your response.

"It is not what happens to us that counts. It's how we respond. Each of us is going to have hundreds and thousands of people 'wrong or hurt me' throughout our life time. Even a life of isolation (the little old hermit in a cabin) will still have people interfering and hurting him. 'It's my privacy. It's my rights. Who do they think they are? How dare they take advantage of me like that. It's not fair. Get off my property.' A constant supply of people hurting him. Injuring his rights. 31

"Wherever I go, people will be abusing me. . . waitresses spilling coffee,. . . cooks who are slow. . . Traffic jams. . .People late for supper. . . People trying to get my money. . . People who are unappreciative. . . People who take advantage. . . People who curse me. . . People who are stingy and out fumble me at lunch so that I'm the one who pays the bill of $6.24. . . Courts which do not appear to do justice. . .Police that won't respond to calls. . . Neighbors that won't keep their dogs and cats at home. . . A mother or father that neglected me, and on and on. A book could be written, listing the numerous wrongs people will force upon me over my life time.

"So the answer is not how to stop these people from wronging me. Let me repeat. The answer is not how to stop these people from wronging me. . . The answer is how to react correctly toward wrongful behavior. . . this is the secret to happiness and peace.

CRISIS—DANGER OR OPPORTUNITY?

A crisis is a situation where things do not go our way. People are not doing what we had expected. My wife forgot to pick my good suit up at the cleaners. Crisis! The car breaks down and stalls on the freeway leaving me stranded. Crisis struck again! The neighbor's dogs get in the flowers. The cats fight at 2:00 a.m. Crisis! I lost a business deal costing hundreds of dollars and many hours of time. Crisis struck again!

Life has from one to as many as a hundred crises a day in store for each person. Avoiding crisis is not the problem. There will always be crisis as long as you can move and breathe. The real issue is how a person RESPONDS to the crisis.

If a person responds to crisis with impatience, anger, anxiety, or rudeness to others, he has picked up the DANGER part of crisis. The danger now destroys his happiness, his health and injures people around who receive the burst of the anger, impatience and anxiety.

Recently I noticed a man at the World Airport; it appeared his luggage was delayed. He went into a frenzy . . . speaking out hate, anger and curses. His luggage was lost. Incompetent help! No one can do anything right anymore! What a sight. The 60 year old acted like a 6 year old.

"As a man thinketh in his heart so is he." Proverbs 23:7.

A grown man that still did not know how to react correctly to a crisis. The OPPORTUNITY part of crisis is to allow yourself a building of patience, selfcontrol and the fruits of the Spirit (love, joy, peace, longsuffering, gentleness, goodness, faith, temperance and meekness).

Begin to recognize the danger part of crisis. Make a conscientious effort to ONLY PICK UP the OPPORTUNITY SIDE OF CRISIS.

Hebrews 12:1 Wherefore seeing we also are compassed about with so great a cloud of witnesses, let us lay aside every weight and the sin which doth so easily beset us, and let us run with patience the race that is set before us.

"Do you see what I'm talking about, Sandra?" I asked.

"Can you explain a little more. It isn't quite clear to me," she responded frankly.

"Well Sandra, you being a Christian and having accepted the Lordship of Jesus in your life, also recognize that Satan does exist, do you not?" I paused for her to respond.

"Oh, yes!" she replied.

"God's word declares that all power has been given unto God. So all real power is of the Lord. The only power Satan has is to deceive, lie, and suggest. Satan does have power of suggestion to other people, making them treat you badly. He can suggest to the other person that they should wrong you.

"Where is the battle then? It is in the mind. II Corinthians 10: 3-5 says, 'For though we walk in the flesh, we do not war after the flesh. For the weapons of our warfare are not carnal, but mighty through God to the pulling down of strongholds: Casting down IMAGINATIONS, and every HIGH THING that exalteth itself against the knowledge of God, and bringing into captivity every THOUGHT to the obedience of Christ.'

"IMAGINATIONS, HIGH THINGS and THOUGHTS are the three things we are to cast down. These are the things which exalt themselves against the knowledge of God. Imaginations, high things and thoughts are in the mind. The mind, Sandra, is the battleground. It is our obligation to cast down these three things. We have control of our thoughts. Jesus said in Matthew chapter six, take no thought of (1) tomorrow (2) food, drink, clothing and (3) making yourself a 'big deal in life.'

"Jesus said, seek ye first the Kingdom of God and His righteousness and all these things (food, houses, position, money, cars, etc.) shall be added unto you. The Kingdom of God is defined in the Bible as not food, nor drink but righteousness, peace and joy in the Holy Ghost."

"Excuse me Mr. Keene, where is that found in the Bible?" asked Sandra.

"Romans 14:17." Sandra had made a note of each scripture I referred to.

"So then what are the weapons in the battle? What are the weapons of our warfare? The verse says they are not carnal but mighty THROUGH GOD to the pulling down of strongholds."

Moving my Bible aside, I located the chalk and rose once again to the chalkboard.

"I'll diagram what these weapons are and what the use of these weapons accomplishes."

SATAN'S WEAPONS PRODUCE	SATAN'S STRONGHOLD
1. HATE	GUILT
2. FEAR	DEPRESSION
3. UNFORGIVENESS	LONELINESS
4. CONDEMNATION (BLAME)	ILLNESS AND DISEASE
OUR WEAPONS THROUGH GOD	
1. LOVE	PULLING DOWN OF ABOVE STRONGHOLDS
2. FAITH	
3. FORGIVENESS	SPIRITUAL MATURITY AND POWER
4. PRAISE	RENEWED MIND
5. SUBMISSION	HEALTHY BODY — PEACE

CAUSE AND EFFECTS

As I sat down I said, "Sandra, I want to teach you something about counseling. Notice the weapons of the enemy. Hate, fear and   35 unforgiveness. The very things that are involved in a broken relationship. If I am deceived into picking up one of these weapons, to fight off a person who is hurting me, I have established a stronghold in my life. A stronghold of guilt, a stronghold of depression, a stronghold of loneliness or of illness and disease. Now we can see why Jesus did not use Satan's weapons when John the Baptist was beheaded. Instead, Jesus picked up one of our weapons, (through God) and pulled down the stronghold! Thereby renewing his mind and elevating his own spiritual maturity. Jesus learned to grow in stature physically and spiritually. We are to do the same. We are to learn to pick up the correct weapons to pull down the strongholds."

Some counselors erroneously instruct clients to pick up the weapon of condemnation and blame. But all this does is to further establish the stronghold of guilt, depression, loneliness, illness and disease in their client's life. They tell me my faulty reaction to people is not my fault. They say my reaction was caused by a father who mistreated me when I was young. My problem, they may say, is caused by a mother who didn't spank me. A mother who abandoned me, or because I grew up in a depressed neighborhood. Blaming and condemning some one else for my problem. Transfering blame to others.

"Let's put a balance scale on the board to demonstrate how blame and condemnation 'appear' to pull down a stronghold but actually does not".

After erasing the chalkboard, I drew a balance scale and put guilt, depression and loneliness on one side.

"The person is out of balance with so much guilt, depression and loneliness. If the stronghold gets too heavy the scale will eventually lower. When the scale tips, a short is created. The person may have a mental relapse, a nervous breakdown, or a serious mental emotional disorder. They lose sight of reality. Life is no longer real. Reality is too painful so the person slips into a life of unreal problems. Hallucinations, snakes, nightmares, excessive fears now dominate the person's life. Thoughts are no longer controlled by the person, but by Satan. Emotions are now out of control. The person may not be able to control his will. He may not be able to control his body.

"Blame and condemnation is used by some counselors to adjust this scale. They put blame and condemnation on the right hand side of this scale. The weight of the blame and condemnation will lift the guilt, depression and loneliness up so that there is a balance.

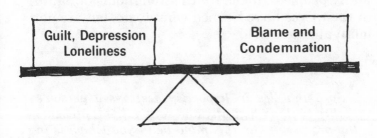

"For a while this appears to work. Blame mother, father, sister, blame the boss, blame someone, blame anyone, blame the ex-husband or ex-wife but don't blame me.

"There is no real success in using this type of counseling therapy. The client often ends up in worse condition. She has just used another of Satan's weapons (condemnation and blame) and it will not pull down the stronghold. It only adds to it.

" 'Judge and condemn and ye shall be judged' Romans 2:1 'thou judgest another, thou condemnest thyself; for thou that judgeth doest the same thing.'

"Condemnation and blame is evidence of a guilt ridden man. He must blame to balance his guilt. Finding fault, criticizing others in an effort to balance their own guilt. Blame and condemnation are all in the same category.

"But blame and condemnation do not eradicate the guilt, depression and loneliness. To be successful we must use our weapons through God to pull that stronghold down.

"I have a reason for spending so much time explaining these things to you. I want you to understand how broken relationships work. I also want to motivate you to take action. It's up to you to act.

"As you act through God, strongholds will fall. Many people burdened with strongholds of Satan in their lives have learned what to do, but are not motivated to act.

SEARING THE CONSCIOUS MIND

Speaking lies in hypocrisy destroys a person's ability to think logically and rationally. It prevents the process of "let this mind be in you which is in Jesus Christ".

Our mind is divided into two areas. The conscious and the unconscious. The conscious part of our mind deals only in reality discovered by our five senses (touch, taste, smell, hearing and sight) and the revelation from God.

The unconscious part of our mind deals in fantasy. We dream (nightmares or day dreaming) in our unconscious mind. Our conscious mind is put to rest while we sleep. When the conscious mind is asleep all sorts of weird, strange, perverse, unrealistic, gory, scary things come to us through the active unconscious mind. These unrealistic dreams seem realistic at the time because the unconscious mind does not possess the capacity to sort out the "ridiculous and unreal".

When we awaken from sleep, the conscious mind is activated again, and begins to KICK-OUT and reject the silly things that were accepted by the unconscious mind.

This is why, when remembering a dream, we forget it about as fast as we can recall. The conscious mind is rejecting those unreal thoughts which were accepted in the dream as fact.

So our conscious mind becomes a safeguard to prevent hallucinations, day dreams, weird thoughts and such that are given to us by Satan through our unconscious mind.

Human Mind

Deals with reality | Deals with fantasy

Conscious Mind | **Unconscious Mind**

What does all this have to do with searing the conscious mind and Christian living? Read with me I Timothy 4: 1 and 2 "Now the Spirit speaketh expressly, that in the latter times some shall depart from the faith, giving heed to seducing spirits, and doctrines of devils; Speaking lies in hypocrisy; having their conscience seared with a hot iron."

SEARING is to make insensitive as I once discovered when I put my forefinger on a hot stove. Pzzz. . . the flesh was seared. The forefinger lost its sensitivity. I could stick the seared flesh with a pin. This further injured the finger, but I felt no pain. The pin in the finger was injuring me, but there was no message to tell me to react to avoid this injury. My finger was seared with a hot iron.

SPEAKING LIES IN HYPOCRISY also sears the conscious mind with a hot iron. The conscious mind can no longer kick out or reject the fantasy that was accepted by the unconscious mind.

Fears, hallucinations, snakes, demons, conspiracy, perverted sex desires, dreams and violent acts that have no reality, become torment in every day life.

I will never forget standing in an Oregon jail cell watching an inmate. He was screaming, yelling and in a state of terror. "The snakes are getting me! Get them off my neck!" He was pulling and clawing at his neck. Tearing his flesh with his nails.

"There are no snakes," I reported to him in sympathy.

He could not hear, but only continued to fight the imaginary snakes that his unconscious mind said were there. Somehow with alcohol, lies, or giving heed to doctrines of devils he had seared his conscious mind.

His God-given safeguard was seared and of little use to him now. That is a terrible way to live. I will never forget the sympathy and helplessness I felt for this man.

Speaking lies in hypocrisy destroys the God-given safeguard of the conscious mind. The garbage comes on through.

SEARING THE CONSCIOUS MIND

How do we speak lies in hypocrisy? Here are some examples:

A. There is a popular "faith confession" teaching that says CONFESS YOU HAVE NOW what does not really exist. By your confession, God will supply the physical result. For example: "Bless God. . . I have a new airplane. It is mine. I can see it now." There, of course, is no airplane. He has no airplane. He is speaking lies in hypocrisy which begins to sear his conscious mind. Fantasy and unreality begins to sneak through and becomes mixed with daylight activity.

If this speaking lies in hypocrisy continue this so called "faith-man" becomes a "fantasy-man".

B. The end justifies the means.

Some Christians believe and practice the art of exaggerating miracles, stretching stories, or making lies to excuse their behavior, all in the name of winning-a-soul. The lies (the means) is justified by the winning of a soul (the end). This Christian is paying a high price for his the "end justifies the means" philosophy.

41

You see he is speaking lies in hypocrisy and thus searing his own conscious mind. Destroying the very thing that God provided for him to ROOT OUT the garbage that comes into his thinking.

Small wonder that preachers, pastors, ministers, counselors and Christians find their later life ministry unfruitful and unrewarding. The spirit of bitterness, the spirit of criticism and the spirit of fear become constant companions in later years.

C. The philosophy that lies are okay as long as they are white lies.

There is a notion that is going about the world of psychology and even Christianity that it is acceptable to tell a person a little lie to make him feel good, or to ease the pain of facing up to reality.

The Bible says speak the truth in love. A lie, whether black or white, small or large, given with good motives or not is a lie, and will sear the conscience of the person speaking the lie in hypocrisy.

As a counselor don't be hesitant to divulge the truth and effect of lies upon the mind to the person who is indulging in such activity.

Notice the scriptures gives a second way the conscious mind may become seared.

Giving heed to seducing spirits and doctrines of devils, horoscopes, fortune tellers and other such activities as outlined in Deuteronomy 18:10 sear the conscious mind. The fantasy and torment of unreal thoughts plague the life of people active in such things. Stay simple in matters of evil and speak the truth.

D. Speaking lies to rationalize and justify one's conduct is prevalent in the world also.

Counselors are tempted to speak lies to ease guilt. Take the blame off the shoulders of the person with the guilt. No matter what the cost. As a Christian counselor please do not fall into this trap. For those who have tried this method of therapy to ease guilt, bear witness that the end is worse than the *beginning.*

Facing the truth is painful but the long range result of accepting responsibility for conduct truthfully is worth the "ouch" that is voiced when that tooth is pulled.

"Therefore to him that knoweth to do good, and doeth it not, to him it is a sin." James 4:17 Knowledge alone is of little value. But. . . act upon that knowledge and it becomes wisdom. Dealing wisely in the affairs of life. Proverbs says that wisdom has more market value (selling value) than silver and gold. A good way to invest in your future is to lay up wisdom. Putting action to your knowledge produces wisdom.

"The only way to capture a man is to get him to think like you do. Ideas capture men. Win a man's mind and you have him. Capture his thoughts and you control him. Man is a product of this thinking.

"Adolph Hitler learned that man is a product of his thinking early in his public life. Get a man to hate, fear, condemn and not forgive with you and that man becomes a SLAVE OF THE STRONGHOLD. Hitler's propaganda was designed to enslave people by changing their thinking. 'Hate the Jews, Hate the Jews. They are inferior,' he declared. On and on he went until the German people were thinking like him. Hate and unforgiveness are a result of broken relationships. A stronghold in the mind of a man that will enslave him. He cannot escape. Every place he goes he must take the enslavement with him. The stronghold follows."

EFFECTS OF BROKEN RELATIONSHIPS
Thursday at 11:40 a.m. Tom became angry with his employer, Ernie, and stormed off the job. Tom found other employment and still will not speak to Ernie.

Tom has a broken relationship with Ernie.

If Tom allows this broken relationship to remain, he can expect to begin seeing evidence of the EFFECTS of Broken Relationships in his life heretofore. What are the Effects?

1. Tom's WISDOM will begin to deteriorate. He will over the months and years to come, experience decisions where he more frequently makes the wrong choice. Wisdom is defined as: The correct action applied to existing knowledge.

Tom may retain his knowledge, but the correct action applied to the knowledge will decrease.

If this broken relationship is allowed to exist for a sustained period of time, Tom can expect to make many costly embarrassing "blunders" in the years ahead. I John 2: 9, 10.

2. The second effect of the broken relationship for Tom is the loss of PROSPERITY and the loss of ANSWERS TO HIS PRAYERS.

"And whatsoever we ask, we receive of him (God) because we (Tom) keep his commandments, and do those things that are pleasing in his sight and this is his commandment, that we should believe on the name of his son Jesus Christ and love one another, as he gave us commandment."

Maintaining a life with no broken relationships and getting your prayers answered are often times synonomous. There is a balance between no broken relationships and answered prayer.

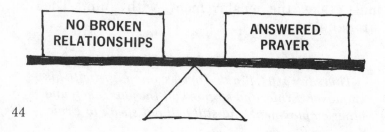

As Tom breaks relationships with Ernie, he upset the balance scale and answered prayer began to decrease.

Understand, I do not define prosperity as money, property, position and power. Ownership of such things usually does not spell prosperity. In fact the reverse is usually true. The more money, power, influence, position and property one has the less he is prosperous.

H. L. Hunt, the deceased billionaire from Dallas, Texas said "A man is not prosperous if he knows how much money and property he owns."

What I mean by prosperity is righteousness, (right relationships with God, others and self) peace and joy in the Holy Spirit. Broken relationships destroy this peace and joy and fellowship with God and others.

3. The third effect Tom can expect from his broken relationship is a deterioration in his HEALTH. All men are made in the image of God and are not designed to harbor and absorb un-God-like activity such as broken relationships.

And God said, "Let us make man in our image after our likeness. . . . So God created man in his own image." Genesis 1: 26, 27.

Most of our body is run by our automatic control center in our brain (automatic nervous system). This center automatically controls our heart. You do not have to tell your heart to beat. It would be ridiculous to have to say, "Beat heart!, come on beat again and again."

All of our vital organs, heart, lungs, kidneys, stomach, colon, glands and so on are controlled by this automatic control center in our brain.

God also built within us, God-like creatures, an automatic self-healing system. You cut your finger and this automatic self-healing system immediately begins to take action. . . to send out corpuscles that *kill germs and other necessary action to begin healing the cut.*

Cancer, flu, tuberculosis, polio and a host of other dread diseases are on your skin; possibly in your food, yet you don't get sick! Why? Your automatic self-healing system is working for you, provided you follow God's system of Balanced Living with no broken relationships.

To allow a broken relationship in a God-like creature such as Tom, is like sabotage to a very delicate instrument. The thoughts that accompany a broken relationship adversely affect the automatic control system.

Stress, anxiety, guilt, nervousness and other such emotions that accompany broken relationships upset the internal organs and reduce health and longevity. Illness often follows broken relationships. The medical world is discovering that more than fifty percent of all illnesses are directly related to our emotions.

The emotions of a man are controlled in part by the effects of broken relationships. Do you want to be healthy? Don't tolerate broken relationships in your life.

4. The fourth effect of broken relationships is a loss of FRIENDS.

It's not much fun to be around people who are experiencing the misery of a broken relationship. They criticize, they complain, they gripe and cast blame on others. A spirit of gloom and bad-news follows them . . . pushing away potential friends.

5. The fifth effect of broken relationships is a failure to MATURE. A person tends to stay childlike and locked in at the age he was at the time of the broken relationship.

Suppose a 10 year old girl is abused or neglected. This may imprison part of her so that she has difficulty maturing, and will often cry and behave like a 10 year old even after marriage, 25 years later. She can't seem to grow past that stage. Steps to free such a person from this condition will be demonstrated later in this book.

"Mr. Keene, I had no idea broken relationships were so significant. I've been so busy concerning myself with everyday life I haven't learned some of these things. Whow! I am becoming motivated to act! And how!" Sandra responded, "I am sorry I interrupted, please go on."

"People with serious broken relationships often can think of little else but that broken relationship. They are continually justifying their own acts. They are continually finding fault with the person with whom they have the broken relationship. It's not much fun to be around people who are so blame oriented, who criticize and complain about places, circumstances and people in their life. We must learn to respond correctly to hurts and wrongs done to us."

SITTING ON A TACK

When I was in the third grade at the age of nine years, I was sabotaged by someone who put a tack in my seat. As soon as I sat down I felt pain. I was hurt.

I had two choices. Number one, I could sit there and continue to experience the pain.

Number two, I could get off the tack and stop the continual injury to my bottom.

As a third grader I chose number two. Get OFF the tack.

If you have a condition in your life that is functioning much like a tack and that condition is causing pain—get OFF the tack. Get rid of the condition. Be as smart as a third grader.

47

"Yes, I see that now, Mr. Keene. But what about real serious wrongs done to a person? Wrongs that hurt so bad you can't forgive even if you try. What about those? Like my former boyfriend lying to me about marriage just to get privileges. How do I get this unforgiveness out so that I can effectually relate to my husband today?" Sandra asked.

Sandra was now ready to proceed. "Alright let's go to step number 3:

Ask God's forgiveness for your reaction and ask God to help you forgive.

"Do you remember the verse said 'the weapons of our warfare are not carnal, but mighty THROUGH GOD to the pulling down of strongholds'? God will back us up if we submit to him and seek his assistance. Jesus was, and is a healer. He healed the sick, the lame, the blind, the deaf, he delivered people who had need and would humbly submit to him. He will do that now with the hurt you still feel from that old relationship. Jesus is the same yesterday, today and forever. I call this 'Healing the Hurts.' As an act of your will, do you forgive Buddy for the way he wronged you?" I asked Sandra.

HURT TAPES

*Your mind is like a giant **IBM** computer that records everything that occurs to you. Events are recorded whether you realize it in your consciousness or not.*

If you were abused or hurt by someone as a child, and that injury has not been healed, your mind can re-run the IBM tape of that hurt over and over again. Unless there is a healing of the hurt, the hurt tape will re-run hundreds and thousands of times during the course of your lifetime.

Each time the hurt tape is re-run it hurts anew. Often hurt tapes create more pain in later life than the pain of the original injury.

Hurt tapes created by father and step-father who molested you, people who spoke harshly or abusively to you. Hurt tapes created by the neglect and rejection of a person in responsibility such as a teacher or guardian. Hurt tapes created by the love-failure of classmates in school such as people belittling; making fun, ridiculing, and harassing you. People excluding you unfairly.

Many hurt tapes are created in teenage years by boyfriend-girlfriend relationships as in Sandra's case. Often by parent-child love failure.

Many hurt tapes are created in later life by abuse, neglect and cruelty within the marriage. People carrying hurt tapes from one marriage to another. The hurt needs to be healed.

Taking the hurt out of the hurt tape does not eradicate the memory of the incident, but it no longer "hurts" to think about it again. The hurt tape becomes only a tape of little or no consequence to you. Most people you counsel with will have hurt tapes that need healing. It is often necessary to deal with them first as was done with Sandra.

When some of the most prevelent hurts are healed the person can then begin to successfully deal with   49 *the development of a disciplined life that leads to establishing peace, joy and righteousness here on earth. The putting off of the old man (old unsuccessful behavior patterns), and putting on of the new man (new response patterns to crisis) then becomes meaningful.*

CUMULATIVE HURTS are hurts piled upon hurt; until the person hurt becomes insensitive to life. They will not and can not show much emotion. They lose the ability to express how they feel. They may become NUMB. The hurts have accumulated. As one hurt is healed other hurts will be exposed so that they too may be healed. See REPRESSED EMOTIONS found later in the book for a technique to expose and resolve cumulative hurts.

"Yes, I do forgive him," Sandra responded quickly.

"I'm going to pray in a moment and Jesus is going to go back in time and heal that love-failure caused by Buddy.

"The Bible tells us in chapter 5 of James verse 13-16. 'Is any among you afflicted? Let him pray. . .

" 'Is any sick among you? Let him call for the elders of the church; and let them pray over him, anointing him with oil in the name of the Lord:

" 'And the prayer of faith shall save the sick, and the Lord shall raise him up; and if he have committed sins, they shall be forgiven him.

" 'Confess your faults one to another, and pray one for another, that he may be healed. The effectual fervent prayer of a righteous man availeth much.'

"Sandra, the Bible tells us that the spirit of a man will sustain his infirmity; but a wounded spirit who can bear? That is Proverbs 18:14. Your spirit is hurt. It needs to be healed so that your 50 spirit can sustain everyday problems as they come along. A healthy spirit can sustain tremendous problems. A wounded hurt spirit can sustain very little. People who get irritated easily, often have a wounded spirit.

"You have confessed your fault of resentment that still hurts your spirit. I would like to obey the verse I just read to you and anoint you with oil in the name of the Lord."

"Yes, please do. I need to be healed," Sandra answered.

Cloetta handed me the small bottle of oil. I removed the tiny lid, spilled a few drops on my fore finger and gently applied it to Sandra's head, just above her eyes. It trickled a little and ran slowly down on her face.

"Take my hands Sandra. Let me gently hold both of them. For you see I can tell what is going on inside through your hands. Relax Sandra. Just relax. Enter into a state of physical, mental and spiritual rest. You have done all you can do. You have, as an act of your will, forgiven him. Now relax and submit, so that Jesus can do his part to pull down that stronghold inside you. Let him heal your spiritual injury.

"When we cease from our own works we enter into the 'rest of the Lord'. Hebrews chapter 4 tells us that faith cannot operate while we are in a struggle. A child non-swimmer cannot be saved from drowning unless he stops struggling. A small child cannot receive the love of a parent while the child is struggling. Relax and let the Lord take the hurt away.

"Jesus will heal you. Sometimes he heals instantly; sometimes he heals slowly over the next several weeks. But nevertheless, he will heal you if you believe and trust him.

"Do you believe the Lord is going to heal that

hurt for you, Sandra?"

"Yes," she replied in a whisper.

Through her hands, I could feel her relaxing. I could almost feel the peace move into her spirit.

"Do you submit yourself to Jesus and trust him, Sandra?"

"Yes," she replied.

"As I commence the prayer you listen to my prayer. As I pray you agree. Because the Bible says 'where two or more agree in my name then I will be in the midst of them and they shall have whatsoever they ask.' Matt. 18:18-20."

Cloetta bowed her head and began to pray softly as I began:

"Father in the name of Jesus, I ask you to now enter into the very spirit of my sister, Sandra, and heal that hurt. Jesus, you are the same yesterday, today and forever. You were there when this hurt was created, the love-failure, Lord, that created this hurt, you saw it and we ask you now to heal. Supply your love Jesus, so that there will be no love-failure. So there will be no hurt. Jesus, Sandra and I both forgive Buddy for his failure. We ask that you also forgive him. Thank you Lord for your faithfulness to me as I submit my entire life to you. Forgive me for harboring bitterness and unforgiveness toward Buddy. Lord Jesus, I receive your healing this very moment. Praise God! Thank you Lord, Hallelujah!"

Sandra was trembling. As she sobbed I knew a healing was taking place. With tears rolling down her face she looked up with a new fire and sparkle in her eyes. Her cheeks were a healthy rose color. She appeared to GLOW all over. She looked like an angel. I asked her, "Sandra, can you hear me."

She smiled and nodded her head with one deliberate gesture.

"Can you talk", I added.

She replied in a mellow drawn out fashion "Yes. . ."

"Is the hurt gone? Did the Lord heal you?", I asked.

"Mr. Keene, while you were talking before the prayer about the weapons, our mind, and broken relationships do you know what I discovered?"

I responded by shaking my head, no.

"I discovered I had a broken relationship with Richard, my husband. I had not forgiven him for the way he had rejected me. So while you prayed, I also asked the Lord to heal that hurt and love-failure. . . And do you know what?". . .

Again I responded with a negative gesture. I knew but in no way wanted to ruin the joy she was about to share.

"He did heal me. He healed me of both hurts from both men.

"Oh, Mr. Keene, I am just bursting with love. Love for the Lord, for healing my hurts. But especially love for my husband. I can hardly wait to get my hands on him. Praise the Lord!"

STEP NUMBER TWO IN COUNSELING
CONFESS THE WRONG

Confession is the only way to eradicate guilt. Blame will not do it. Don't try to shift the blame to others. When a man's folly brings his way to ruin, his heart rages against the Lord.

It is man's own stupidity which ruins his life, yet he is bitter against the Lord. It is important to understand that bitterness, disappointment, sorrow, and misery come from our own stupidity. Other people do not make us bitter and miserable regardless of what they do to us. It is our problem from our incorrect response.

By responding incorrectly we hurt ourselves. And yet man, in his rebellion, not only rages against others, striking out with blame while excusing himself, but ever since Adam and Eve he has raged against the Lord.

When God confronted Adam with his disobedience Adam declared, "Lord, the woman which you gave me, she is the one who gave me to eat of the fruit." The woman then shifted the blame to the serpent.

The fact that others have done much to shape our lives is a fact. However, each individual must bear personal responsibility for how he allows others to influence his conduct. No one can blame others for his bad behavior, even when he has been taught that behavior from childhood. What he learned may be unlearned. . . since we may reshape ourselves.

We are responsible to confess our faults and allow Jesus to heal these hurts and assist us in reshaping our lives.

THE SPIRIT of a man is continually crying out "confess, confess, confess so that I might be healed".

THE MIND of that same man says "Don't confess, don't confess, don't confess. You'll make a fool of yourself and be punished".

Confession ministers to the spirit of a man. This is why a person feels so good in his spirit when he confesses and gets his wrongful behavior OFF HIS CHEST. This is the reason a polygraph (lie detector) works. The spirit inside will not tolerate a lie without reacting so that the reaction can be detected in body

54

functions (heart beat, perspiration, etc).

Sandra has confessed her fault of unforgiveness toward her old boyfriend Buddy. We have prayed and anointed with oil and can expect Sandra to receive a Spiritual healing of her hurt. This hurt has been the root of many of Sandra's frustrations. She tells of explosive anger. She tells of anxiety and despair. The root cause is the hurt by Buddy and Richard.

"I'm happy for you Sandra. The Lord has healed the love-failures and taken the 'hurt' away. You feel very joyous. You are excited about your healing. But listen to me carefully. The excitment will subside in time. You need to know the other steps to assist you as Satan attempts and suggests that you are not healed.

"Step number 4: Forgive yourself for harboring bitterness."

I moved back to my chair. "Women are very guilt prone. Being a woman, Sandra, you are subject to this. In other words, women feel guilty easier than do men. The susceptibility of women to feel guilt is often used by men to manipulate. I have seen women by the scores come into my office for divorce. Many early admissions were 'it's all my fault'. Upon inquiry I found the husband was drinking heavily, not working, coming home drunk, chasing other women and at the same time telling his wife 'it's all her fault'. She soon would examine herself so closely, she found a weakness. She would then accept the fault cast upon her by her husband. She was convinced she was at fault. After all, the husband declared it so, and she could see where she was at fault. She now had guilt. She is miserable.

"I learned at the age of four years, that women have an easy inclination to feel guilt. One cold afternoon my parents would not let me go outside. I wanted my own way. I looked at my father and said, 'If you don't let me go outside, I'm going to run away!'

"Dad simply stated, 'You'll get cold and hungry and soon come home.' He went back to reading his book.

"I then turned to my mother and said, 'If you don't let me go outside I'm going to run away!'

"She looked sad and forlorn, so I added, 'And the mean old lion will get me and eat me up. Then you'll be sorry! It'll be your fault I'm dead'.

"A tear came to her eye, she reached down, picked me up and said, 'It's okay little Leonard, you can go outside. Get your coat and I'll help you put it on.'

"I grinned, scurried for my coat, and then headed outside having found the door to getting my own way with a woman. Cast guilt on them and you can get anything you want. It was not until I was a little older that I discerned that the guilt I cast on a woman; whether it was my mother, my sister, my friend or my wife is to the injury of that woman.

"Women can't take much guilt. They must learn to dispose of guilt or they will burst. I have since

56

learned to guard my conduct so that I will not injure women by the use of guilt, especially against my wife.

" 'Likewise, ye husbands, dwell (live at home, not at the job) with them according to knowledge (get to know her) giving honor (not abusive of your position) unto the wife, as unto the weaker vessel and as being heirs together of the grace of life; that your prayers be not hindered.' I Peter 3:7

"The wife is the weaker vessel. She can't hold much. A weak vessel has weak walls. It will burst if it gets too full of guilt, hurt or loneliness. How does a woman empty her vessel? Talk. . . talk. . . talk. . .

"A woman needs to talk regularly. She needs to confess her faults to her husband to cleanse her conscience. If the husband does not listen, she is more susceptible to the glib tongue and listening ears of a scoundrel whose sole desire and aim is to get her into his bed. The guilt from wrongful conduct (lying, cheating, stealing, adultery) rests the heaviest on the women. Remember, women are the weaker vessel.

"Sandra, realize that you are guilt-prone and that you need to regularly eradicate any guilt. A good way to forgive yourself is to step up to a large mirror at home. Look yourself straight in the eye and say 'Sandra, will you forgive me for harboring bitterness against Richard and Buddy?' Now answer, 'Yes, Sandra, I forgive you.'

"Confess your fault to your husband so you can acquire a good self-image, the I accept Sandra, I accept you attitude.

HUMILITY AND THE SELF-IMAGE

There is a relationship between humility and a good self-image.

As we increase humility on the scale we also increase our own good image of self. What is humility? It is being known for what I am and not being ashamed or arrogant about it.

Letting people look at the inside of me. Letting people see I have weaknesses and hurts inside just like everyone else. As I expose my insides, I also expose my goals and motives. If I'm to OPEN-UP I have to clean up selfish and evil motives. I have to give up "making myself a big deal".

People who refuse to open up and be humble often fear exposure of wrong goals, hurts and weaknesses. Explain this concept to this person. Truth given in love is a mighty force in counseling. Open your hearts to God and others.

You be the example in the new openness. Ephesians 5:21 says, "Submitting yourselves one to another in the fear of God."

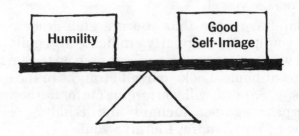

"Now don't concern yourself again with that former condemnation of self. Forgive yourself and be done with it. Any questions on that point?"

Sandra shook her head "No" as she looked up from her writing.

"Okay, Step number 5: Confess aloud 'I forgive. . .' (Insert the name of the person you are forgiving).

COUNSELORS ARE EXAMPLES

A counselor's life must be in correct order to administer truth to others. The old Indian adage "White man speaks with forked tongue" is more prevalent today than ever. As my son Randy once reminded me. "Dad," he said, "your action speaks louder than your words."

Many ministries are not fruitful because their homes are not in order. With an unloved, neglected, abused wife at home, rebellious children and finances in a mess the so called counselor begins to tell the wounded walker how to live successfully.

The wounded walker can see through this smoke screen of pretended qualities and declares to himself, "No thanks Mr. Counselor, If your advice is not working in your own life, it probably won't work for me.

"Besides, I believe I have less problems than you."

Titus 1:5-9 says "For this cause left I thee in Crete, that thou shouldest set in order the things that are wanting, and ordain elders in every city, as I had appointed thee; If any be blameless, the husband of one wife, having faithful children not accused of riot or unruly. For a bishop must be blameless, as the steward of God; not self-willed, not soon angry, not

59

given to wine, no striker, not given to filthy lucre; but a lover of hospitality, a lover of good men, sober, just, holy, temperate; Holding fast the faithful word as he hath been taught, that he may be able by sound doctrine both to exhort and to convince the gain sayers."

Jesus preached and showed the Kingdom of God Luke 8:1. Jesus spoke and demonstrated by his orderly and controlled life the goodness of the Kingdom of God. People could see the Kingdom of God (peace, joy and righteousness) on the inside of Jesus. His words carried life.

Do your words carry life to the wounded people? It is time we Clean Up Our Act and look like Christians, act like Christians, and experience our inheritance like Christians.

Let the wounded people come into your home to see how well you have these principles working in your life.

"Step number 6: Ask forgiveness from those you have wronged and hurt.

"Is there a stumbling block in the path of one of your former acquaintances because of you. . .? Does someone hate or dislike you? Does someone hold resentment toward you? A direct confrontation is necessary. Telephone calls or letters seldom work adequately.

"Matthew 5:23, 24 'Therefore if thou bring thy gift to the altar, and there rememberest that thy brother hath aught against thee; leave there thy gift before the altar and go thy way; first be reconciled to thy brother, and then come and offer thy gift.'

"Your gifts to God in the form of money, property, time, talent or praise are of little consequence if you have aught (a broken relationship) with another person. It is small wonder so many ministries bear corrupt fruit. They have not cleaned up their past relationships. Husband and wife arguing and fighting on the way to Sunday School. As they put their 'Pepsodent Smile' on at the church door the aught against their brother is still in their heart. Why doesn't God honor my worship? Why doesn't God honor my gifts of praise, money and time? Man cannot love God and hate man. If you truly love God you will mend all broken relationships. If you do this your gifts at the altar will be meaningful.

"I knew a man who had a broken relationship with a co-worker. They faced one another every day but would not speak nor let their eyes meet. This went on for six years. Finally one of the men moved away. As far as I know both men are still enslaved with this broken relationship. Asking forgiveness for your wrongful conduct usually will be returned with a statement similar to this. 'Oh, you should be the one forgiving me. I wronged you badly. I should be the one asking forgiveness.'

"Sandra in your case you would be ill-advised to seek out the old boyfriend. Don't re-activate that relationship by returning to him. The Lord has healed you. You can pray for him so that the Lord can begin to help him. However, you should go to your husband and ask forgiveness for your attitude toward him. This will help make your husband more sensitive to your delicate womanhood. Even though you were only five percent at fault, still ask his forgiveness.

"Make certain you follow the commandment of Ephesians speaking the truth in love. Not the truth in bitterness. Read and study all of Matthew chapter 18. Make certain you and the Lord have purged out all the bitterness."

Sandra spoke up with a quick, "Why?"

"Because bitterness can be tasted by the other person. Bitterness is bitter! It turns people away. Make certain your speech has no bitterness, your action has no bitterness, and particularly your attitude has no bitterness.

"For guilt, depression, loneliness, and bitterness all show up on one or more of these three levels— our speech. . . our action. . . or our attitude.

SPIRITUAL COVER

Often a person's problem stems from a failure to understand and maintain Spiritual Cover. A home church, a shepherd, a family order with the Husband in authority and the Wife in submission is necessary to keep the wolf away.

The parable of the hundred sheep in Matthew 18:11 demonstrates this graphically. The wolf goes after the one lone sheep who by his rebellious nature wanders off from the protection of the fold, therefore, vulnerable to attack. The parable tells us the shepherd follows the lone sheep. I can almost visualize the shepherd taking his crooked cane and beating the wolf away from that lonely beat up sheep. . . the wolf bites at the heels and snaps at the ears of the lone sheep. The shepherd pleads for the sheep to re-submit to the fold. The shepherd says, "Please come with me, back to the fold. You'll be safe and protected there."

For you see, the intersubmitted—subjected relationships of the sheep in the fold protects each sheep from Satan, who as a roaring lion, goes about seeking whom he may devour. I Peter 5:5-8.

"Mr. Lone-Sheep, please submit yourself to the fold. Don't be afraid. We won't hurt you."

Submission requires that the lone sheep be humble toward the other sheep. Verse I Peter 5:5 says we are therefore CLOTHED WITH HUMILITY.

This clothing of humility protects and covers each sheep in the fold from the wolf and the lion.

In my experience as a counselor most people in need of guidance and help would fit into the lone-sheep class. What are the reasons for leaving the fold? They range from greed and selfishness, to hurt and injury. Greed for self or hurts from other sheep. It is the counselor's responsibility to motivate the LONE SHEEP to return to the fold. I have found the most successful way to motivate is to explain this concept of entering into close relationship again. People get weak and weary from the harassment of the wolf.

It is then that we must be bold, and rescue with truth. For the truth sets us free from the bondage of doing our own thing.

"Humble yourself therefore in the sight of God and He [God] will lift you up." James 4:10.

How do I humble myself in the sight of God? Humble yourself in the fold by submitting and subjecting to other brethren and by doing so, you have automatically humbled yourself to God. It is then that God's grace begins to give you spiritual cover and protection. Brother, open yourself to one another. Enter into close relationships.

"Likewise, ye younger, submit yourselves unto the elder. Yea, all of you be subject one to another, and be clothed with humility; for God resisteth the proud, and giveth grace to the humble. Humble yourselves therefore under the mighty hand of God, that he may exalt you in due time; Casting all your care upon him;

63

for he careth for you. Be sober, be vigilant; because your adversary, the devil, as a roaring lion, walketh about, seeking whom he may devour." I Peter 5:5-8.

"The Lord tells wives to submit yourselves to your own husbands as unto the Lord. To submit means 'to open your arms' to receive the love from the husband. To fit into the husband's plans, to adapt yourself to him. Sandra open your own arms. Stretch them out wide. Notice that all your vital organs are exposed. Your face, your heart, your stomach, your lungs and your reproductive organs. When a woman submits to her husband she exposes these vital organs to him. When a husband fails to love his wife correctly he injures her.

SUBMISSION   THE HURTS

"When a husband 'rejects' his wife it is much like the husband taking a knife and stabbing her in the vital organs. What happens when your arms are open in a submitted stance and someone slugs you in the stomach? Your arms immediately close. You receive a hurt. Your arms close to protect yourself. This is what a woman does when a husband abuses, neglects, or rejects her. A love-failure on the husband's part injures the submitted wife. She begins to close her arms for protection. Continued

64

abuse, neglect and rejections will close her arms of submission until she is no longer submissive. When a wife is not submissive with open arms she cannot receive love. Too many hurts. . . 'I can't trust him'.

"What you have been doing Sandra, is learning about these things and allowing the Lord to heal those love-failures so that you can once again open your arms in submission to your husband. Love will pass by if the intended receiver is not in the correct submitted stance.

"Let's draw a picture of the submission." I went to the chalkboard and began to draw as I explained.

THE EFFECT   **THE HEALING**

SUBMISSION

Glancing at Cloetta I walked back to my chair. Cloetta motioned toward the coffee pot and I nodded "yes". As she refilled my cup and Sandra's I went on talking.

"Sandra, keep your spiritual arms of submission open long enough for your husband to love you."

Often it becomes a matter of teaching a husband to love his wife. Many husbands do not realize the complexity involved in loving their woman. Loving a wife is more than just having sexual relations with her on occasion and bringing money home to pay bills.

A woman must be loved 24 hours a day. Not just 30 minutes occasionally. Loving her includes picking up clothes and turning off the television to listen to her describe trivial things regarding the home and the children. Women need to talk. A husband needs to learn to be a good listener to allow his woman to empty her "weak vessel" so it will not burst.

Loving a wife includes bathing and shaving on your day off. Treating her special on Saturday, rather than golfing with your best friend. A man truly becomes a man when he makes his wife his best friend. Continually wooing and loving her in small things. Mowing the grass, fixing the fence are all interpreted by women as an expression of love.

Whose responsibility is it to see that the husband and wife relationship stays intact? Some say it is both. Husband and wife. They say husband and wife share equal responsibility to keep the marriage intact. Well, in a way I suppose that is true. But the problem usually ends with both husband and wife "blaming" one another for not pulling their load when difficulty arises.

66   Some say it is the woman's responsibility to keep

the marriage intact, because after all, she is the homemaker. They say it is her job to submit to the husband and the trouble begins when women fail to submit. But I found this also not wholly correct. Most women want to submit to their husbands. Most women do submit to their husbands with "open arms". But men, not knowing how to love a woman, or men not even realizing they should learn to love their women have rejected, neglected and abused them.

The wife then pulls back, closes her arms of submission to protect herself and the marriage becomes nothing more than an arrangement to get the kids raised. The wife has found she can't trust her husband, so she begins to lead. The wife now leading the marriage, and like Eve she will eventually be deceived. Instead of heaven on earth, it becomes hell on earth. When the wife is in leadership the husbands want to stay away from the conflict at home so they play golf, take out of town jobs, work extra hours or build a boat. Anything to avoid the conflict that occurs when the roles of husband and wife are reversed.

I believe that it is the husband's responsibility to see that the marriage stays intact. It is his responsibility to see that outsiders and foreign objects (bitterness) do not separate the relationship. It is the husband's job to stop a wild beast attacking the marriage. . . To stop another man from seducing his wife. . . To stop anything that might divide the husband and wife relationship. It was Adam's sin when he allowed Eve to be deceived by Satan. Adam was held accountable.

Genesis 2:24 says, "Therefore shall a man leave his father and his mother, and shall cleave unto his wife; and they shall be one flesh." The man is always in motion. He is leaving one place and 67 going to another. In the man's relationship, he is always leaving his father and mother and moving toward his wife. Moving toward her in a continual effort of pursuit. A pursuit to establish the husband-wife relationship as one flesh. The man is the aggressor. He is the one who seeks out the female, (his wife) to establish the "one flesh". The man is the aggressor in sex activity, protection, providing and leading the family.

THE HURRY, HURRY SYNDROME

This syndrome often destroys a person's sensitivity. And of course, sensitivity is a key to effective relationships.

In my studies, I've found the people in a hurry, are often the people who need counseling and therapy in later life. Especially, there is a need for counseling those people who live around the man in a hurry. Why? A man or a woman in a hurry breaks relationships with other people. Others are offended; others are hurt; others are injured by this man in a hurry. The guilt and effect of the broken relationships shows up in later life.

It's much like a red Washington delicious apple from Tacoma, that you have kicked with your foot and bruised. This bruise is not apparent because the skin of the apple was not broken. But the apple was bruised inside by the kick. For the next few hours the bruised apple appears to be a non-bruised Grade A apple, worth at least 25¢. However, with the passing of time, a dark brown and black spot becomes apparent on the surface. If the results of this injury are not cut out and removed, it will soon contaminate and destroy the entire apple. The apple will become useless and of no value. Much the same thing happens in broken relationships with people. If these broken relationships are not healed and solved they will contaminate and render useless the people involved.

Proverbs 19:22 says, "He that hasteth with his feet sinneth". Why? He steps on people and breaks relationships. Man is not constructed by God to run 120 m.p.h. continually. If he does he will soon run out of gas. Heart attacks, ulcers, colitis, respiratory illness, early death, broken marriages and juvenile delinquencies in children are often the plight of the 40 year old man in a hurry. Slow down, men. Else you leave another rich widow behind.

Learn to pace yourself so you can climb the entire mountain. The first time I climbed Mt. Pitt in Southern Oregon I learned this lesson. It was six miles to the top. The first two miles I almost ran, anxious to conquer the mountain. Our guide said, "Slow down or we'll bury you along the route". We climbed the mountain one step at a time. Slowly, but surely. Never in a hurry. Pacing and conserving our energy for the full climb. Husbands, lead your families at a slower pace.

Just as the Lord continually woos man with love asking for more submission unto him; so a husband must continually woo his wife with love. As she begins to trust him, she slowly opens her arms of submission to him. As she submits, she receives the husband's love. The more the husband woos and loves her the more she trusts him. As she learns to trust the husband she opens further her "arms of submission" to him.

"They shall be one flesh", the verse says, "and the man shall CLEAVE unto his wife." CLEAVE MEANS to fasten together. Like a button in the button hole. The button is not much by itself. Neither is the buttonhole. But as the button actively seeks out the button hole, "woos" it into submission, a relationship is established. The button and the button hole have become one. They are fastened together. A one flesh, one shirt concept. Pull on the garment from both sides. The garment will tear before the union of the button and button hole will separate.

Husband cleave unto your wife. Fasten yourself together, so that no outsider including bitterness and resentment can separate this relationship. It is your responsibility. You see that the husband-wife relationship is securely cleaved (fastened) together as one flesh.

Husband you are accountable to God as head of your home for the success of the relationship.

"What therefore God hath joined together let no man put asunder" (separate). What therefore God hath joined together let no husband allow to separate. We as husbands are accountable to God for this relationship. It was Adam's sin when Adam allowed Satan to intervene in the marriage. It will be the husband's sin if he allows a third party and/or problems to separate the husband and wife relationship.

HUSBAND FASTEN YOURSELF TO YOUR WIFE

WIFE ADAPT YOURSELF TO YOUR HUSBAND

REJECT, NEGLECT, ABUSE; the three enemies of submission. The three things that stop a wife from the "open arms of submission". When the arms of submission close, the wife no longer can receive love from the husband.

A vessel must have the lid off to receive. A vessel must be submitted to be filled. Rejection, neglect, and abuse put the lid on the vessel. The vessel is no longer submitted. The lid is on the vessel to protect it. It cannot receive the wine. As I pour the wine it hits the lid and spills down the side. Wasted.

"Sandra, the Lord has taken the lid off your vessel so that you can receive again the wine (love) of your husband. The Lord has healed the love-failure caused by Richard. It was the neglect, the rejection and the abuse of you that caused you to automatically close your arms of submission for protection. You couldn't receive the occasional love offered by Richard because you were not submitted. The Lord has healed those love-failures. This healing is a slow process but as you are healed, spiritual submission will allow you to once again receive love from your husband. Learn to adapt yourself to your husband. Learn to look to him as your shepherd."

"But, Mr. Keene, how will Richard learn that a husband's neglect, rejection and abuse stops a wife's submission? What will stop him from injuring me again?" Sandra asked.

"Sandra, I want you to begin to speak the truth in love toward your husband. Tell him honestly how you feel. Before the Lord healed your injuries you could not have done this. You would have spoken the truth in bitterness." If there is bitterness and resentment (caused by an injury from neglect, rejection or abusive conduct) in a wife's spirit, the husband can detect it. He can actually taste the resentment. It's bitter."

71

When we eat something that is bitter we spit it out. That is exactly what a husband does when he tastes the bitterness in his wife's attitude, action or speech. He spits it out by more abuse, more neglect and more rejection of the wife. Sometimes it's by a blow to the head. Sometimes he curses her. Sometimes he just vanishes.

"But Sandra, now the bitterness is gone. You can speak the truth about your feelings to him. You can begin to expose your thoughts. You are beginning a new age of communication to become one flesh! As you express yourself in love toward Richard, he will become more aware of your delicate nature. He will become more sensitive to your submission. Begin to admire him. Men need to be admired by their wives. In due time explain broken relationships to him. Or, if you feel led of God, have him come in, perhaps I can talk with him.

"He will learn to stop abuse, neglect and rejection if you begin to speak your feelings to him in love. Not just your bad feelings, but also your good emotions. Particularly, your good feelings. Begin to expose your love for him in words, in action and in your attitude. God will now begin to deal with him."

"Mr. Keene, is there anything else that I can do to make my husband aware that he needs to love me more tenderly. That he needs to fasten the relationship together in one flesh?" Sandra asked.

"Read Ephesians chapter five with him. Don't instruct him. Let him lead. The Lord will reveal the truth to him in time. Be patient. You may want to describe this counseling session to him. He will begin to see that the Lord has returned you to a submitted position to receive his love. 'Hurry,' the Lord says, 'love her while there is still time. Love her as I loved the church. Love her as I love you. I gave my life at the cross for you.' Husband, you

72

also give your everything to your wife. Especially your time and attention. If a man earns $100,000 a year at his business, and is mayor of the city but is a failure at home, he is a failure in the eyes of God. No man wants to fail. God will show you both how to communicate with one another. Submit yourselves one to another to receive one another's love."

EPHESIANS 5

"Be ye therefore followers of God, as dear children: And walk in love, as Christ also hath loved us, and hath given himself for us an offering and a sacrifice to God for a sweet smelling savour. But fornication, and all uncleanness, or covetousness, let it not be once named among you, as becometh saints; Neither filthiness, nor foolish talking, nor jesting, which are not convenient: but rather giving of thanks. For this ye know, that no whoremonger, nor unclean person, nor covetous man, who is an idolator, hath any inheritance in the kingdom of Christ and of God. Let no man deceive you with vain words; for because of these things cometh the wrath of God upon the children of disobedience. Be not ye therefore partakers with them. For ye were sometimes darkness, but now are ye light in the Lord; walk as children of light; (For the fruit of the Spirit is in all goodness and righteousness and truth;) Proving what is acceptable unto the Lord. And have no fellowship with the unfruitful works of darkness, but rather reprove them. For it is a shame even to speak of those things which are done of them in secret. But all things that are reproved are made manifest by the light; for whatsoever doth make manifest is light. Wherefore he saith, Awake thou that sleepest, and arise from the dead, and Christ shall give thee light. See then that ye walk circumspectly, not as fools, but as wise, Redeeming the time, because the days are evil. Wherefore be ye not unwise, but understanding what the will of the Lord is. And be not drunk with

wine, wherein is excess; but be filled with the Spirit;
Speaking to yourselves in psalms and hymns and
spiritual songs, singing and making melody in your
heart to the Lord; Giving thanks always for all things
unto God and the Father in the name of our Lord
Jesus Christ; Submitting yourselves one to another
in the fear of God. Wives, submit yourselves unto
your own husbands, as unto the Lord. For the
husband is the head of the wife, even as Christ is the
head of the church; and he is the saviour of the body.
Therefore as the church is subject unto Christ, so let
the wives be to their own husbands in everything.
Husbands, love your wives, even as Christ also loved
the church, and gave himself for it; That he might
sanctify and cleanse it with the washing of water by
the word. That he might present it to himself a
glorious church, not having spot, or wrinkle, or any
such thing; but that it should be holy and without
blemish. So ought men to love their wives as their
own bodies. He that loveth his wife loveth himself.
For no man ever yet hated his own flesh; but
nourisheth and cherisheth it, even as the Lord the
church; For we are members of his body, of his flesh,
and of his bone. For this cause shall a man leave his
father and mother, and shall be joined unto his wife,
and they two shall be one flesh. This is a great
mystery; but I speak concerning Christ and the
church. Nevertheless let every one of you in
particular so love his wife even as himself; and the
wife see that she reverence her husband."

I looked at Cloetta and said, "Could we have one more cup of coffee?"

Cloetta smiled, slid out of her chair and moved toward the doorway as I stood to erase the chalkboard. Then she spoke, "There are pastries in the coffee room do either of you want a snack?" She stood waiting at the door for our reply.

"Something very small," Sandra said.

Cloetta looked at me, she was sure my response

was going to be yes. I smiled and nodded in affirmation.

As Cloetta left to prepare coffee and snacks I thought to myself, we have become so professional in our counseling that we tend to set time limits on each session. Appointments scheduled back to back. One hour or one-half hour sessions do not produce much fruit. The client no sooner gets settled down from the activities and fear of life, and it is time for him to leave. No time to build a relationship, no time to confess faults, no time to forsake bad behavior, no time to anoint and pray and not enough time to teach how to enter into close relationships with others.

Remembering back to the hundreds and hundreds of clients I've counseled, I thought, the real success cases came from the counseling session when we had unrestricted time alloted to the first session. Two or four hours in the first session. Then only a few phone calls in follow up to solidify the results of the session. Although nervous and upset, a person is more open to receive during that initial session. The client has submitted to the counselor. Submitted to receive assistance for a problem that cannot be solved by the client. The client has tried everything. Now she needs your help.

She possibly has talked to people and family, read books and spent hours in anxiety looking for an answer, all to no avail.

FIXATIONS

How a person views a situation can be hindered by a "fixation". If a person has a "they will hurt me fixation" he will interpret many situations as a threat to his well being. The threat is real in his thinking; even though there is no real danger in fact.

If I was riding in your automobile, while you were driving, and you heard me yell out "Look out for the truck", you would feel threatened if by past experience you had determined that trucks do indeed, collide with cars. You have been conditioned to respond to such alarm. This conditioning was established from experience or knowledge imparted to you by other situations. Many people have a "salvation fixation". They have heard salvation by Jesus so often they are conditioned to respond with alarm and with a loud "No thanks".

The message is a threat to their being. Or, in the case of some Christians who read all of the Bible with a "salvation fixation" interpreting most verses as directing man to heaven. Or other Christians who have a "faith" or "money" fixation.

They have such a fixation on money that when they read the word "Give" in the Bible the words money, money, money echo in their minds. Their fixation on money has hindered their ability to discern the Bible verse the way the Lord intended. For example, some people with incorrect motives and goals could easily read Luke 6:38 "Give and it will be given unto you" as meaning money, money, money without giving thought to the fact that "Give" is a verb and the noun or subject of the sentence must be located. Without a money fixation a person can easily go to the previous verse and find out what the writer is referring to give.

Be ye therefore MERCIFUL, as your Father also is merciful. JUDGE NOT, and ye shall not be judged; CONDEMN NOT, and ye shall not be condemned; FORGIVE, and ye shall be forgiven. The subject of the sentence is to be merciful, not judge, not condemn and to forgive. It has nothing to do with money or property. In fact the writer of Luke was a physician, a doctor, of his time. He was not a financier, or a man of God giving some secret to getting rich.

Many people who seek your counsel will have fixations. Fixations that hinder their ability to discern life and circumstances.

It takes patience and re-education to dispose of these many fixations. A common fixation encountered by counselors is that of wrong goals.

People who love self so much that all life situations are analyzed on the basis WILL THIS BENEFIT OR BE A PROFIT TO ME. This is a "Self-fixation". It often deters genuine friendship and creates selfish, lonely people. The people with self fixations usually experience frustrations, guilt and confusion in later years of their life.

The client is at the end of her rope. Desperate. Crying out in a submitted spirit for help. This initial two to four hour session is often the best time to get to the problem. Occasionally a few clients receive benefit from the time spent in counseling in future sessions. To understand the reason for this it is necessary to understand the concept of Ears-to-Hear.

"Take heed what ye hear; with what measure ye mete it shall be measured to you; AND UNTO YOU THAT HEAR SHALL MORE BE GIVEN. For he that hath to him shall be given; and he that hath not, from him shall be taken even that which he hath." Mark 4:24, 25.

A client comes for counseling expecting to receive help, expecting to receive help in a certain area of his life. Help to the extent and to that degree they have submitted to the counselor and have 'Ears-to-Hear'. The counselor must discern this area of submission in the client and aim his advice and counsel at that area. For it is only in that area that the client has "Ears-to-Hear". If the counselor fails to discern that critical area of submission, the client will not receive, no matter how artful and articulate the counselor instructs and guides.

77

For example: Joann came to me. She was in trouble with the law. There was a warrant out for her arrest for an over drawn bank account. She wanted help. She submitted to me and had ears to hear concerning solving her legal entanglement. I could detect from her conversation that Joann had more serious problems. She had several broken relationships that were bothering her. I also could detect she was over extended in her activities. She was just too busy. So busy with work, recreation and friends that she had no time to mentally step aside, stop and re-examine her life. She needed to stop to see more clearly where she was going and why she was going there. My target area as counselor was to hone-in on the area of submission where Joann had ears to hear, her legal problem.

As I began to hit this area with my counsel, her ears to hear were receiving, and much like the verse says "and unto you who have, shall more be given", her area of submission quickly increased, so that we were able to move into areas of business and broken relationships.

If the counselor misses this target area of submission, the client will not receive, but often becomes irritated and closes up the small area she had allotted to have ears to hear. A diagram will illustrate this.

Some clients arrive at the office totally submitted. They are so desperate, they have ears to hear in all areas. But generally speaking it starts with the one limited area. As soon as the counselor locates that area and begins to minister, the client learns to trust the counselor. As trust and ears to hear develop and expand into larger areas, the counselor can also expose and cover more of the problem.

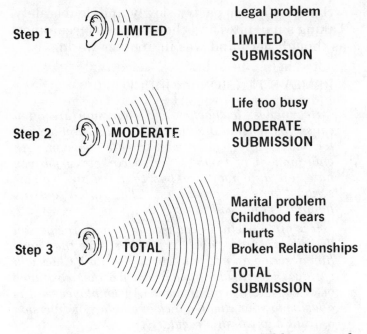

Step 1   LIMITED

Legal problem

LIMITED SUBMISSION

Step 2   MODERATE

Life too busy

MODERATE SUBMISSION

Step 3   TOTAL

Marital problem
Childhood fears
     hurts
Broken Relationships

TOTAL SUBMISSION

The door opened as Cloetta quickly entered carrying a tray of coffee and several delicious looking pastries.

There was a spirit of excitment in the air. Not just the excitment about coffee and pastry but the excitment of the "light" and the "healing" that was taking place in Sandra's life.

I looked at my $10.00 Timex. It was exactly 4:00 p.m. We had been in conference two hours. Look what progress we had made. I wish all cases would progress at this speed. People need help so badly. So many are suffering at the hands of one another. People continue to suffer because of a fear of more injury if they "open-up" to another human being. Fear of exposing our hurts, guilt, motives and weakness. Ashamed, not knowing whether the person we open up to will stab us in the stomach with a knife or make fun and ridicule our weaknesses.

Sandra ate her pastry slowly and deliberately. Taking small bites and chewing each piece almost as though her mind was in another world.

REMOVE TENSION PRODUCERS

Headaches, backaches and confusion are often caused by tension producers. The television blaring for hour after hour can create tension. An environment of troublesome co-workers, a job you hate, an automobile or bus that irritates can be serious tension producers. They often destroy happiness and lead to early death.

It is often useful in counseling to have the person describe an entire day, hour for hour. After that, have him describe an entire week, day by day. Clues will surface that will identify a problem of overwork, lack of sleep, wrong employment. An employer that is abusive to your client, a lack of a hobby or diversion or failure to worship regularly.

Don't think counseling has to be so professional and highly introspective that everyday practical solutions are not used. All problems are not solved by digging deep into the past. The present environment is as often as not the cause and the cure.

We all sat quietly for a few moments, then Sandra spoke, "I must settle something in my life before I leave here Mr. Keene. I feel a need to really open up and tell you what I feel on the inside. I sense you will understand and be able to help me."

"Go ahead and talk Sandra. Tell me whatever you like. I'm here to help." I replied.

As she began to talk, I thought of the submission the Lord was talking about in I Peter 5. As we submit to one another we are clothed (covered) with humility, and the mighty hand of God begins to cover and protect us from Satan, who as a roaring lion goes about seeking who he may devour. Satan is looking for the lone-sheep, the unsubmitted sheep. The one sheep doing his or her own thing. As the lone-sheep gets torn, injured, bit, kicked, abused, a crusty wall of fear attaches itself around the spirit of that "sheep." The crusty wall of fear prevents outsiders from entering. It also prevents the real you from exposing the weaknesses and hurts inside. This crusty wall of fear around Sandra's spirit has begun to crumble. She now wants to really expose some of her inner hurts and weaknesses. She trusts me not to laugh or further injure her.

We have begun building a relationship that is salty. The relationship has loyalty and trust as a main ingredient.

Sandra was talking softly, "I have never really thought of myself as having many fears. But I am beginning to see where my worries are really fears.

"When I worry about something happening to Richard I can see it really goes back to when I was always afraid something was going to happen to my Dad. I always had a hidden fear that one day he might be killed coming home. Where this came from I really don't know, except maybe from hearing my parents fight.

"Fighting over money or drinking. And knowing my Dad was a fast driver and did at times mix drinking and driving. One time when my parents were fighting they called me in and asked who I would choose to stay with. They of course, did not divorce and all the trouble, outwardly at least, was soon forgotten. But they failed to pass the news on to us kids.

"It is confusing as a child to see so much hate, and then to see them getting along. Sort of like the song 'The Games People Play'. I now see that it is not really a game, but hurts. Unless they

81

understand hurts as you have explained to me, they will be plagued for life. I really see where they, like myself, have to desire the hurt to be removed, seek inner healing and in my case build a good relationship with my husband. Then and only then, the hurt becomes a remembrance and not pain.

"My parents were good people and I'm sure in no way intentionally hurt us. I always felt second best, even though I was the oldest. My brother was sick a lot, and all the money he had to have spent on him, and all the attention made me want to be sick also. I sort of inwardly thought, someday I'll get sick and you'll have to baby me.

"Money was another problem. Someone always spending too much. I guess that is why I try so hard never to complain about money. I saw how it divided relationships.

"As a child I was very quiet. I had a speech problem when I started to school. At school the kids would get me to say something then laugh. Even when I answered roll call they laughed. They may have been laughing with me, however, I was not laughing. So I just drew back.

"One time in Junior High we were passing around our year books for signatures. I overheard one girl ask whose book she had. The girl next to her answered, 'Oh, the girl that never talks or does anything.'

"That answer caused me to cry myself to sleep that night and many nights thereafter. It really did hurt because I always thought I was just being polite. Anyway, that thought had helped me justify my not talking and not expressing my emotions to others.

"We moved my last year of high school and I had to talk. The kids in the new school didn't know I was quiet and never talked. They asked questions and I answered. It was a small school so there was no getting lost in the crowd. Now I probably talk too much.

"I still do not like large crowds or totally new crowds. And I do prefer to be in the background.

"I really believe in the Bible where it says a woman is not supposed to talk in church or to teach men. Guess that is why I really want my husband to be the man of the house. I want him strong so I can be behind him. So he will make the decisions, protect me, and love me.

"Knowing I don't have to be sick to be loved, talk lots to be loved, know all about money, news, investments or anything else. Just be loved and taken care of. Knowing each night he'll come home. I guess, what I really want is to become the one flesh you talked about.

"I want to have a family some day. And I want them to have good parents. Ones that they will be proud of.

"Now that I talk about it, I guess I do have fears. Sometimes I wake up at night trembling. Sometimes I get fearful during the day when I'm alone. Afraid the elevator will stick and leave me alone between floors. Mr. Keene, are these fears caused by the fear of my youth? The things I just told you about? I'm an adult now, how can I still be hung up over childhood fears?" she ended with a deep sigh.

REPRESSED EMOTIONS

Unlike Sandra, not all clients are willing to express their emotions. In fact many people find it difficult or impossible to express their inner feelings. We can call these repressed emotions. Let us take an illustration. Suppose Alice at age 4 years, is left at the babysitter 83 *while Dad and Mother go to a party. Alice is told her parents will return at 12:00 midnight. At 2:00 a.m. she awakes from her nap at the babysitter and says "Where is my Daddy and Mommy".*

The sitter explains, they have not returned. Alice cries. The sitter tells Alice that "Big girls don't cry". Don't express the emotion of hurt or disappointment. It's not grown-up-like. At 6:00 a.m. Alice again awakes at the babysitter and says, "Where is my Daddy and Mommy". The sitter explains again that "Daddy and Mommy have not returned".

Alice feels rejected again. Again she begins to cry and weep expressing the hurt that is on the inside. She misses her parents. Her parents lied to her. There is hurt and pain. The pain that is almost unbearable. The pain that feels like a knife in her stomach. Again the sitter reminds Alice "Big girls don't cry. Go back to sleep."

The implication is that she should not express the hurt that is inside her. Alice can't stop herself, she cries expressing the hurt uncontrollably. The sitter gets angry and further rejects and rebukes Alice.

When Mom and Dad finally do come at 10:00 a.m. Alice runs to them with open arms and crying. Both parents tell her "don't cry. We are here now. Be a big girl. Don't cry". She learns to repress emotions such as hurt, despair, anger, guilt, and frustration as not being adult and lady-like. If these emotions are not expressed and dealt with they are never disposed of. These unexpressed emotions stay inside Alice and torment her. She begins to accummulate more unexpressed emotions, she represses them down. Inside the fear of exposure mounts up until Alice doesn't dare let us see what is on the inside, as we may declare her to be childish, unlady-like, weak, or sick.

What does Alice do? She closes up and does not allow people to see on the inside. Alice has repressed emotions from hurts. Alice can never truly be happy and enter into peace, joy and righteousness until these emotions are vented and confronted.

Modern life styles demand men and women be strong, courageous, loners and not express emotions. So few people have close relationships in which they can vent their feelings. Remembering that most people who come for counseling are loners, we can begin to see the importance of Step Number One in counseling. Develop the relationship.

With the hurried life style there is more need for close relationships than ever before.

The most successful method I've found to assist "an Alice" to release these repressed emotions and begin building a relationship with another human being is to use the Sentence Completion Exercise. I present several phases, the beginning parts of sentences, which are to be finished by the client with the first words entering her mind that constitute a completion of the sentence. When the client expresses willingness to cooperate I explain the procedure as follows.

I will say the first part of a series of incomplete sentences. As spontaneously and as quickly as possible, you will reply with the first set of words that occurs to you that complete the sentence. Avoid worrying about the rightness or wrongness of your response. There are no right and wrong answers. Avoid editing and censoring your reply. I'm simply interested in the first response that occurs to you. Never mind if the response sounds foolish, ridiculous, illogical or the exact opposite of your beliefs. Just relax. Don't try to make anything happen. Don't try to second guess or analyze. Just let what happens, happen. Here is an example. I will say, When I look at the mountain you might say "I see snow and trees".

Here is a list of incomplete word phrases that can be used to get the feelings started.

1. When I get up in the morning. . . .

2. As a woman . . . .

3. Sometimes I feel . . . .

4. I don't understand myself when . . . .

85

5. *Why do I always* . . . . .

6. *Whenever I try* . . . .

7. *I want* . . . .

8. *I can't tolerate* . . . .

9. *Weakness to me means* . . . .

10. *If I give into my feelings* . . . .

11. *Sometimes I want to cry out* . . . .

12. *When people look at me* . . . .

13. *Why do people so often* . . . .

14. *God is* . . .

15. *When I look in the mirror* . . . .

16. *Ever since I was a child* . . . .

17. *I feel safe when* . . . .

18. *Mother was always.* . . .

19. *She always expected* . . . .

20. *She never* . . . .

21. *That made me feel* . . . .

22. *And it also made me feel* . . . .

23. *Father was always* . . . . .

24. *He never* . . . .

25. *He always expected* . . . .

We can never feel forgiveness for an emotion we will not admit having. It is difficult to confess to God an emotion we do not confess to ourself. This test will assist people who have not been accustomed to venting emotions, or facing up to them.

26. *When I made a mistake* . . . .

27. *Men to me are* . . . .

28. *Women to me are* . . . .

29. *Being alone to me means* . . . .

30. *Pleasure to me is* . . . .

31. *Freedom to me means* . . . .

32. *If I ever let out my anger* . . . .

33. I don't dare show my anger because . . . .

34. Sometimes I push my thoughts away because. . . .

35. Sometimes I want to cry out . . . .

36. Sometimes I feel guilty . . . .

37. The thing I'm most tired of is . . . .

38. To me worship is . . . .

39. Sometimes I push my thought away . . . .

40. If I were more emotionally open . . . .

41. It's hard to be emotionally open because . . . .

42. Being hurt means . . . .

43. If I ever admitted I really needed another person. . . .

44. I cut myself off from everything because . . . .

45. When I admit I'm in love . . . .

46. To submit means . . . .

47. I can remember . . . .

48. Commiting myself means . . . .

49. I can't do that because . . . .

50. If I didn't always have to protect myself . . . .

This is not an exhaustive list of phrases and you can add to it as the client opens up to you in areas of concern. As they begin to confess and express the repressed feelings and emotions they will find they can more adequately confront their problem. It is often useful to tape record your counseling sessions and let the client take a tape home to listen and study his responses to these phrases. A free interchange with another human being is the objective. An interchange of the hurts and the weaknesses on the inside so that the Lord may heal and repair earlier damage.

"Sandra, a crusty wall of fear around your spirit created during childhood, has prevented you from fully maturing. Physically you are mature, but not inwardly. That wall of fear stunts the growth of certain characteristics. If we are emotionally hurt or put into great fear as a child, it begins to create this wall of fear (and hate in some cases) around your personality. The personality is not allowed to mature or grow as the body grows. The body goes on to advanced ages 10, 20, 30, 40 and so on but that phase of the child remains the same age. Reliving the same emotional hurt.

"An example would be, in your case, the people making fun of your speech, your parents fighting, or reliving the same fear of your parents separating and you losing one or the other. Your fear of being left out and alone. That part of you has not grown up. There is still a portion of you that is a little child. A little child still hurt and fearful. Am I right?" I asked.

"Yes, I know you are right," she replied with a sheepish grin on her face. "When I remember these things about myself I often get tears in my eyes. I sometimes cry. People ask me why I'm crying. I tell them I don't know. I'd feel dumb saying I just thought about my childhood or something out of my childhood. Could it be the little child in me crying from the fears and hurts?" she asked as tears once again begin to well up in her eyes.

"Exactly," I replied. "Let me draw you another diagram. Let's make a circle and pretend that circle is the real you. Now, as you were hurt and subjected to fear as a child, a wall began to build up around the REAL YOU. You got so you would not trust people entirely. The wall began to exclude people from your life. In part, the little child in your past is now a loner. You don't show her to anyone for fear of criticism and further hurt. She is alone, unsubmitted.

Real You

Crusty wall of fear prevents exposure of the hurt-weak child-like character inside.

Unexposed hurts weaknesses inside

"Sandra, do you find yourself speaking, understanding and thinking as this hurt child inside of you? Does it appear that she sometimes controls your behavior?" I asked Sandra that question slowly not wanting her to be afraid and not answer.

"Yes, I believe so. Sometimes I don't act very mature. Even I can see that I am acting immature so I know other people can see it," she returned cautiously.

"That little child is in prison. We are going to begin the process of freeing her. Paul in I Corinthians 13:11 says 'When I was a child, I SPAKE as a child, I UNDERSTOOD as a child, I THOUGHT as a child; but when I became a man, I PUT AWAY CHILDISH THINGS. For now we see through a glass darkly (we do not see or understand life because of this bound up child) now I know in part; but then shall I know even as also I am known. And now abideth faith, hope, charity these three, but the greatest of these is charity (love).' "

Laying my Bible back on the corner of my desk I went on.

"Through the love of Jesus we can let him go back and heal the love failure and fears of this child. This bound up child will be set free by the love of our Lord. So that you can PUT AWAY CHILDISH THINGS. Just like Jesus healed your heart from the broken relationships, he will heal the fears and hurts of this child.

"Chapter 14 in I Corinthians verse 20 Paul says, 'Brethren, be not children in understanding; howbeit IN MALICE BE YE CHILDREN, but IN UNDERSTANDING BE MEN.' "

I stood, taking the eraser, I began erasing the crusty wall of fear diagram and began printing in bold print. Sandra was beginning to write so as not to miss anything.

A. CHILD IN BONDAGE

UNDERSTAND AS A CHILD/fear

MALICE OF A MAN/hate and
**   unforgiveness**

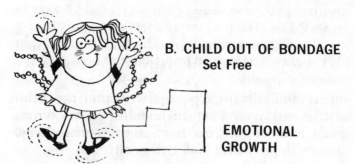

B. CHILD OUT OF BONDAGE
Set Free

EMOTIONAL
GROWTH

UNDERSTAND AS A MAN/no fear

MALICE OF A CHILD/no hate or
**   unforgiveness**

"The healing power of Jesus will move you from A to B. He will set free the yoke of bondage of that little child." I moved back to my chair slowly.

Large tears began to roll down Sandra's face. She began to speak, "Jesus is healing that little child in my past right now and we haven't prayed yet. Oh, I love the Lord." The presence of God began to fill the room. Joy permeated all of us. Her body and spirit glowed with excitement. The Lord was healing that little child in bondage, so that Sandra could now understand as an adult and not as a child. She could now be freed of that fear and insecurity that was a carry-over from childhood.

"Thank you Lord, for healing Sandra. Praise God! Praise God! Thank you Lord." Our voices were all in one accord giving thanks to our Heavenly Father.

Then it was quiet in the room. Tears were streaming down Sandra's face and across her cheeks onto her neck. She was not even aware of the tears as they dampened her clothing about her bosom. The power of God was all over her. God was healing his child. Sandra had submitted to God and allowed him to heal her. What a picture!

James 5:16 says "Confess your faults one to another and pray one for another, that ye may be healed. The effectual fervent prayer of a righteous man availeth much." Sandra had confessed to another we had prayed and God had healed. What a glorious sight!

It is so important to confess what is on the inside of the real you. The weaknesses, hurts, wrong goals, fears or guilt. So that a submitted brother or sister can pray and God can heal.

It is important at this juncture to notice that James is talking to Brethren in verse 12 who are in relationship spiritually to one another. Confession should only be to close, submitted brethren (believers in Jesus Christ). Confession to casual Christians usually causes trouble not healing. People not in submitted relationships often use information from such confession for gossip and as a vehicle to belittle or criticize the person.

CONFESS AND FORSAKE BAD BEHAVIOR

"He that covereth his sins shall not prosper; but whoso confesseth and forsaketh them shall have mercy." Proverbs 28:13.

"Confess your faults one to another and pray one for another, that ye may be healed. The effectual fervent prayer of a righteous man availeth much." James 5:16.

Confession should be limited to one person you are in close relationship with, which would include a counselor. . . spend one or two hours of time to build a trust relationship. A person who is suffering, will receive healing and mercy if they follow these steps.

1. Submit to one of the brethren to help you

2. Confess and admit faults

3. Forsake and/or stop the bad behavior

4. Pray one for another and anoint with oil

Confession pushes out the guilt of the wrongful behavior.

A criminal act must be confessed by the person commiting it. Some people are driven by guilt to police authority so that confession can take place. The guilt leaves, but unless the other three steps are

*taken the result is only short lived and the person is
back into wrongful conduct.*

*Build a relationship, confess the wrong, stop the
bad act and pray, is the underlying procedure in
counseling that will heal the injured spirit.*

Confession of inner hurts, fears and weaknesses
in counseling sessions is not always possible nor
advisable for some people. Some things are best
confessed only to a husband or wife, a pastor or a
priest. Someone who is loyal and who is possessed
of sufficient compassion to love the person in
trouble. You should become sensitive to entering
into submitted relationships with the people God
sends you. Never show conduct in attitude or
speech that could be interpreted by the counselee
as rejection of her as a person. But don't agree with
the wrongful behavior either.

"Sandra, do you have a close girlfriend about
your same age?" I asked.

"No," she responded with a puzzled look on her
face.

"Is there some woman that seems to be
interested in helping you that you may have
ignored?" was my next question.

"No, I don't believe so," her voice trailed off.
Then she spoke, "Wait. . . . I do believe there
is. . . Mary Baldwin, has always showed a great
deal of interest in me. Could it be that God sent her
to be a close friend and sister to me? A submitted
sister? She does seem so wise in matters pertaining
to God. Come to think about it she is a well-
balanced person. Maybe God did send her to me."

"Sandra, allow God to give birth to the
submitted relationship. Do not push it. Just be
open and it will happen. You and your Christian
friend can both draw strength from the
relationship.

93

"Let me write a list of five rules in developing a submitted relationship." I stood by the chalkboard and while I was talking erased the last notes.

"RULE ONE: BEGIN TO RELAX." I sat on the edge of the desk and explained. "Relax physically, mentally and spiritually. Love cannot be received by a person who is up-tight. Love cannot be received by a person who is struggling. . . . Like earlier when we talked about the non-swimmer and the struggling child. There is a peace, there is a rest for God's people. But as Hebrews 4 says, we cannot enter this rest until we cease from our own works.

"We must re-establish our goals. Stop taking excess thought of (A) food, drink, clothes, shelter, (B) making ourselves a big deal and (C) of tomorrow—the future. Jesus said take no thought of these things. Matthew 6:33 says "But seek ye first the Kingdom of God, and His righteousness; [right relationships with God and people] and all these things will be added unto you.'

"Stop the struggle. Relax and enter into the rest and then you can begin to open up in building submitted relationships. You will not be meeting people just to foster and promote yourself. It is only when you re-establish your goals (cease from your own works) that you will be able to develop a person-to-person relationship that is open. A relationship where the truth can be spoken in love. . . Without fear of wrong motives or selfish gain. True loyalty can be developed. When loyalty is present in a relationship, peace and trust follow."

I moved back to the board and wrote: RULE TWO: BE SENSITIVE TO WHOM GOD SENDS YOU.

"The second step to enter a submitted relationship is to be sensitive to whom God sends to you. You can only have submitted relationships with one to possibly seven people. For most of us, five relationships will be more than enough to occupy our time. A husband, a wife, a child, a pastor, a brother, a co-worker and so on.

"These will be people who will have loyalty that you can discern in their spirit. A relationship that withstands an all night illness. A responsible attitude to the relationship, where your sister sits all day with you, or you with her, if the circumstances demanded.

"Become sensitive to whom God has sent to you. And become sensitive that God also sends you to other people. But remember, you may be acquainted with dozens of people, and see them frequently; but only intimately are you related to a few."

RULE THREE: ACCEPT PEOPLE AS THEY ARE.

This time I moved back to my chair and leaned forward and began to explain the last step I had written on the board.

"To enter into a submitted relationship is to accept people as they are. Don't try to change them. Accept yourself as you are, and accept others as they are. Your motivation, as you enter into the submitted relationship, is to love and help that person. Not to change them. Don't try to control, manipulate or reform them. Accept them as they are so that you can both begin to start being honest with one another. Schedule a weekly luncheon or coffee. Schedule a time you can regularly see one another to develop a trusted relationship. No gossip. Just a real building of a relationship on a one to one basis. You will find that you'll start telling her of your fears. You will find yourself sharing early life experiences. Some of these experiences will expose hurts and injuries that you

95

need to deal with as we have done in this session.

"You have shared a few of those hurts with me. However, you'll find that as you enter a God-inspired-submitted-relationship, you'll expose and receive healing for even more hurts, fears and weaknesses that still may remain. This counseling session has only been a band-aid program to get you by until you can enter into closer, deeper, relationships with Richard and another one or two people.

"It may be God will send a husband and wife to you and Richard to relate to. Whatever, just be sensitive to who it is and do not act hastily. To be sensitive means to be gentle and slow. God will confirm in several ways to whom you are to relate. As you move into relationships with the person, be willing to accept their success and failure.

"Sandra! Don't look at me so strange! Everyone has failures. As you share your fears, weaknesses and hurts what do you think they will be doing? It is a mutual relationship for the good of all persons. They will also look to you for guidance and love. Be open to share and to comfort. Like any new relationship, there is always a honeymoon period. When you and Richard were married did you not have a few months of little or no problems and just exciting joy?" I asked.

Sandra looked toward Cloetta, hesitated for a moment. . .and then sheepishly replied, "Yes and I would give anything to recapture that period of time. What went wrong? We have just kind of drifted apart."

"The answer to that question, Sandra, lies in the fact that God united Sandra and Richard together so that you would each have someone to look to for comfort. You each have NEEDS that are to be met. You both have fears, weaknesses and hurts that need to be dealt with. In part, God sent you to each other for that reason. To meet the needs and to help heal the hurts. After the honeymoon period is over, the relationship will die, unless you both begin opening up and moving into a deeper commitment toward one another. Many people, not understanding the purposes of a relationship, fail to use this opportunity to heal and also heal the hurts of previous life.

"The Lord says in Ephesians 5, even before he tells a wife to submit and a husband to love, both SUBMIT YOURSELF ONE TO ANOTHER IN THE FEAR OF GOD. This opening ourself to one another is a condition precedent to a wife submitting and a husband loving. It must be done first.

"Submitting to one another is done in the honeymoon period. Opening up to one another is begun during the honeymoon period and is a continual process. As husband and wife open up and reveal inner secrets of the hurts, the fears and the weaknesses, the Lord backs them up. You shouldn't try to change one another. You should try to change yourself. You must submit (conform) to one another and the Lord will back you up."

Each time I moved toward the chalkboard to write, Sandra would pick up the pencil so she too would be ready to write.

RULE FOUR: GIVE UP PERSONAL DESIRES FOR THE GOOD OF THE RELATIONSHIP.

I slid back into my chair looked toward Cloetta and then back at Sandra.

"Step number four in building a submitted relationship is giving up personal desire for the good of the relationship.

"When I first married Cloetta she liked to ride bicycles and take walks. I thought bicycles and walking around the block with my wife was 'kid-   97 stuff". Not something a MAN should be seen doing. I discovered after several months of marriage that I needed to give up some of my personal desires for the good of the relationship. Had I not done this the relationship would not have grown."

Sandra looked toward Cloetta and smiled. Cloetta returned her smile quickly and spoke, "I gave up some of my personal desires also."

I smiled, "We all have a deep inner longing for closeness to another human being. If the moment of truth in which to open up, comes in a relationship, and I balk and refuse to open up, I will turn away. I will seek a satisfaction for this inner emptiness elsewhere. Perhaps in my work, perhaps in my play such as golf, football, or tennis. . . supplying a substitute for my need of close friends. If you have balked at opening up, I encourage you to turn back again to the God-given relationship and begin anew.

"If you don't, these fears, hurts and weaknesses will remain with you for life. The Lord has provided this medicine of inter-relationship with one another. Use it. Explore it. Receive the healing. Give up personal desires for the good of the relationship.

FRUITS OF THE SPIRIT

"Mr. Religion" frequently speaks out and declares "Oh brother Keene, I walk in the Spirit".

It sounds good, but before a man can walk in the Spirit, he must learn to live in the Spirit. I believe the next time I'm asked to help select a new pastor for a church from the 93 applicants that were called of God while they were walking in the Spirit I will notify them that we will be sending deacons to live in their homes for a week. This way, we can see if the prospective man of faith and power has really got it together with his sheep at home. I suspect once we notify them of this procedure, 92 of the applicants will notify us of a calling of God elsewhere.

The first three fruits listed in Galatians 5 deal with the self to self relationship (Love, Joy and Peace). Here is where we learn to live with ourself. No inner conflict. As one begins to establish these fruits in his life, he begins to live in the Spirit.

The next three fruits deal with the self to others relationship (Longsuffering, Gentleness and Goodness). Now these are truly fruits of the Spirit that effect other people. These fruits of the Holy Spirit are for the benefit of others.

The last three fruits deal with the self to God relationship (Faith, Meekness and Temperance). Now a man is walking in the Spirit.

If we live in the Spirit, Let us also walk in the Spirit. Let us not be desirous of vain glory, provoking one another, envying one another.

"By the way, I now enjoy walking around the block, riding bicycles and after 16 years of marriage I even enjoy helping Cloetta do dishes, yard work, cook and make beds. Note one thing, I do not need to do these things often, but just be willing to give up my desire to watch television or play golf for the good of my husband-wife relationship."

Sandra stood and spoke, "Could I bring Richard down here for you to talk to him? I want him to have that kind of attitude!"

"Yes, Sandra, I'll talk to Richard. But remember, the wife is the attitude leader or pacesetter. As you set this attitude of giving up personal desires for the good of the relationship, Richard will follow. Men generally follow whatever attitude the wife sets. If she is bitter and grouchy so follows the husband. If she is pleasant and sensitive to her husband, he will tend to follow."

99

RULE NUMBER FIVE: FOR ENTERING INTO RELATIONSHIPS IS TO RECEIVE INNER HEALING AS WE HAVE DONE IN THIS COUNSELING SESSION.

"Before we conclude this session, I want to give you the last step in healing the hurts in your spirit, that have been caused by father, mother, teacher, brother, boyfriend, husband, preacher, friend, etc.

"Let's read Mark 11: 22-26"

Cloetta handed Sandra a Bible opened to Mark. As soon as Sandra found the verse she looked up and I began to read, " 'And Jesus answering saith unto them, have faith in God. For verily I say unto you, That whosoever shall say unto this mountain, Be thou removed, and be thou cast into the sea; and shall not doubt in his heart; but shall believe that those things which he saith shall come to pass; he shall have whatsoever he saith. Therefore I say unto you, What things soever ye desire when ye pray, believe that ye receive them, and ye shall have them. And when ye stand praying, forgive, if ye have aught against any; that your Father also which is in heaven may forgive you your trespasses. But if ye do not forgive, neither will your Father which is in heaven, forgive your trespasses.'

"The point that this step makes is that the answer to your prayers is directly related to your forgiving those people who have wronged you.

"Your prayers are empty if you do not, as an act of your will, forgive these people. People go through 'prayer lines' in healing meetings by the scores expecting to be healed by the Lord but still have these old hurts inside. These old hurts with the accompanying bitterness and unforgiveness often prevent the Lord from answering their prayers.

"I John 3: 22 and 23 also confirm that God will answer our prayers, but we must keep His commandments by believing on Jesus and loving one another. We cannot love one another if we hold bitterness within us. Confess it to a submitted brethren, have them pray and be healed James 5:16."

I looked down at my watch. It was now 5:05 p.m. We had spent 3 hours counseling.

"Sandra, is there anything that comes to mind that you would like to discuss before we adjourn?" I asked.

"All I can say is whoo!! I have never been so bandaged with truth in my life. I am excited. I feel like a new person. I'm anxious to begin doing the things you've told me. But how can I remember all this? Won't I forget?" she asked.

I looked toward Cloetta and she reached, handing me a book.

"Take this book and re-read it. Share it with others. If you have questions please feel free to call us at anytime." Sandra read the cover "PLEASE DON'T HURT ME".

"Now the last step to heal the hurt is to remember to pray for the person who hurt you.

"Shall we join hands and pray?"

FIVE STEPS TO COUNSELING

The discussion with Sandra now covers the fifth step in the five steps to counseling. For review I have listed the five steps below.

1. Build the relationship

   By exhorting

   By comforting

   By charging

2. Confess the fault

3. Forsake the fault

4. Anoint and pray

5. Encourage entry into submitted relationships

EPILOGUE

Two days later, on a Friday evening I received a telephone call from Richard, Sandra's husband.

His first comment was, "What did you do to my wife?"

With some caution I replied "What do you mean?"

"She's a new person. I've never seen anything like it. I've got a brand new wife. It's terrific. What did you do? I must know. Can I come and talk with you?"

I set a time for Richard to stop by.

What Richard was experiencing was the joy that comes from a wife that truly was submitting to his plans and his love. He could detect that his love was now being received by Sandra. Sandra was now fitting into his plans. If Richard decided to move to Alaska, Sandra would go without a hassle.

When Richard stopped by to see me he brought Sandra. What a joy to see two happy people on their second honeymoon. They were both beaming with excitement.

Sandra's last comment was, "Mr. Keene I've never been so happy in all my life. Thank you. Oh, thank you."

My reply was simply, "Don't thank me Sandra. Thank God for his healing power. God heals the hurts and takes the pain away. We are serving a great Heavenly Father."